For Clifford

March 1999

From: All your colleagues
at The Independent

Jeremy Warner

Robert Chalmers

Matthew Rowan

Diane Coyle

Roger Trapp

Lawrence D'Agostino

Andy Verity

Andrew Cornelius

Amy Frizell

Trevor Fishlock

Alister McRae

Phil Thornton.

Francisco
Guerra

Isabel Berwick

angpno (Andrew).

Nigel Cope

THE TIMES
One Hundred Greatest Cricketers

John Woodcock

MACMILLAN

First published 1998 by Macmillan

an imprint of Macmillan Publishers Ltd
25 Eccleston Place, London SW1W 9NF
and Basingstoke

Associated companies throughout the world

ISBN 0 333 73641 9

9 8 7 6 5 4 3 2 1

A CIP catalogue record for this book is available
from the British Library.

Typeset by The Florence Group, Stoodleigh, Devon
Printed and bound in Great Britain by
Bath Press, Bath

Foreword

Is genius something all on its own? Are people born great, do they achieve greatness, or do they have greatness thrust upon them?

In my view, the person we like to call a 'genius' is like ourselves at our best only much more so. The difference between him or her and the ordinarily good performer is a matter of smaller or greater increments – increments in dexterity, in determination, in range, in the capacity to rise above the conditions. Occasionally someone is great because he transforms an activity into something new; sometimes we are inclined to call him great because he does so many things to a level that astonishes us; sometimes it is more a matter of ease and grace; sometimes of superlative courage.

Let me be more specific. W.G., in the words of a great player of the next generation, Ranjitsinhji, '... revolutionized batting. He turned it from an accomplishment into a science. He founded the modern theory of batting by making forward- and back-play of equal importance. I hold him to be the maker of modern batting. He turned the old one-stringed instrument into a many-chorded lyre. And, in addition, he made his execution equal his invention. W.G. Grace discovered batting: he turned its many narrow straight channels into one great winding river.'

The regard was mutual. Here is Grace on Ranji, 'You will never see a batsman to beat the Jam Sahib if you live for a hundred years.' A fellow-player said of him that he moved as if he had no bones. He invented the leg-glance. But his batting 'could not have been merely stylish at the expense of effect,' wrote Scyld Berry, 'for he was the greatest run-scorer of the time. Ranji fulfilled one of the main criteria of any artist ... an artist in the omission of inessentials.'

Here we have two exemplars of greatness in batting: one who created what became the basic elements of technique for ever more; the other who invented a stroke, was wonderfully graceful, and who was effective by means of total simplicity.

The cricketer we call 'great' may earn this term because of his ability to master conditions in which ordinary, first-class players can only struggle, desperately trying to survive. I think of Hobbs, who on good pitches would often give his wicket to the most deserving of the professional bowlers so as to give others a chance, but on difficult pitches, against the better bowlers, knew 'that was the time you had to knuckle down and make a century if you could . . . that was the time you had to earn your living. After all, Surrey paid me to make runs; not just runs when we didn't need them, but runs when we did need them.' Or I think of Compton, whose genius evoked awe in his team-mates: Titmus and Bennett used to say of Compton's innings of 150 against Sussex on a drying pitch at Lord's, out of a total of around 200, that he played shots that you would have said were impossible on such a pitch, against a bowler like Ian Thomson, such as cover drives on the up.

Indeed, the capacity to evoke amazement in fellow-players and spectators alike is one aspect of greatness, though it must be allied with effectiveness and reliability.

So far I have spoken of batting alone. But much of what I have said applies to bowling, wicketkeeping and fielding. For the words 'great' and 'genius', we tend to look for such qualities as development of the art, elegance and economy of style – provided always that this is allied to effect, and to the overcoming of adverse conditions.

I should add some further considerations: range, courage and determination, and consistency.

Range applies most obviously to leg-spin bowlers, but also to the greatest fast bowlers. Warne is a great bowler by virtue of his powers of spin and range combined with tremendous accuracy. Lillee – I think the greatest fast bowler that I faced – could bowl every type of delivery, outswinger and inswinger, off-cutter, fast leg-break and googly, which he combined with accuracy, hostility and a self-belief which kept him going through the longest, hottest days in the field. Range enters even more prominently when we come to the all-rounders. 'The king, the four-in-one,' the West Indian fans called Sobers, the greatest all-rounder of all. Sobers might have appeared in John Woodcock's 100 as batsman if he had never bowled a ball, and as fast bowler if he had batted at number 11. On top of all this, he was a respectable slow left-arm orthodox bowler, a talented bowler of 'chinamen' and googlies and a wonderful fielder.

We are reluctant to allow sheer accumulation and correctness of technique the appellation 'great'; however, these qualities are rightly recognized in Woodcock's list. I think of the likes of Barrington and Boycott. They are included because we admire their attributes so much: the capacity to survive when they, at times, look vulnerable and under fire; their courage; their sheer contribution to winning a match by battling through thick and thin; and the fact that such achievements do not come without rare skills, rarely risked, for reasons of cost-effectiveness, or displayed with full freedom.

Cricket-lovers cannot resist tackling the impossible yet fascinating challenges of selecting the best-ever team, or the greatest bowling attack, or indeed the 100 greatest cricketers in actual order of merit. We may doubt, on logical grounds, the feasibility of ranking in a single list batsmen with bowlers. We may question the predominance of batsmen over bowlers in John Woodcock's top ten. One of the charms of the exercise is that no one can be proved wrong, or for that matter, right. And there are so many imponderables, such as are we to pick on the basis of a career high-point, or of consistency over long periods of time? If the former, there would undoubtedly be a place for Tyson, described by no less a judge than Bradman as, for a couple of years, the fastest bowler he ever saw. If we were to stress the capacity to dominate, together with infinite style, Azharuddin would get a look-in. If uniqueness and the courage to overcome handicap, then Chandrasekhar, stricken by polio as a child, must have been included. Sheer rhythmic power might have lifted Ambrose to a higher rank and have let in Garner. The respective placings of Botham, Imran Khan and Hadlee depend on whether they are remembered at their early peak, or whether more stress might have been given to the last two's evolution into the players they made themselves into in their thirties.

If, if, if . . . Woodcock has laid himself open to differences of opinion with followers of every age and in every region of the world. He has also started hares which will lead his readers a merry run!

Mike Brearley
April 1998

Introduction

In the course of choosing these hundred 'greatest' cricketers, I liked to picture them reaching the same heights whenever they had played. The order in which they are placed, as if on some scholarship roll, is inevitably invidious and essentially provocative. It is integral to the exercise, I am afraid, that all such lists are flawed by sins of omission and commission.

A year or two ago, I watched on television as two former England captains, Ray Illingworth and Bob Willis, and one eminent pundit, Robin Marlar, all dressed up in their evening best, picked their eclectic all-time England XI. Despite Marlar's frantic protestations, the other two withheld their support for W.G. Grace, with the result that by two votes to one the champion of champions was left on the balcony. To me that was like leaving William Shakespeare out of a First XI of English dramatists. It goes to show, though, what an unrelentingly subjective business this is.

When asked how he rated Brian Lara, the West Indian prodigy who had relieved him of the record individual Test score, Sir Garfield Sobers, as generous a soul as ever played cricket, expressed his own very decided views on greatness. 'The word great is used much too often,' he said. 'You can't call Bradman great and David Gower great too. If Gower was great you have to invent a different word for Bradman, who was an all-time great, like Everton Weekes. Ian Botham could have been great but he never was. Greatness is something that comes with time and consistency of performance. There are exceptions. Ted Dexter wasn't around for long, but I thought he was a great player because he never looked in trouble and was always attacking and dominating the best bowlers in the world. I am certain Brian will become a great player, but he is not one yet. He is a potential genius, but they said that of Lawrence Rowe.'

Subsequent events have tended to endorse Sobers's assessment of Brian Lara. However, I don't agree that Botham was not a great cricketer, nor that Lara is a potential genius. To me, Botham was a colossal cricketer and Lara is already a genius, albeit one whose progress towards absolute greatness has been slowed by instability.

Not all cricketing geniuses become great cricketers, any more than all great cricketers are possessed of genius. It is difficult even for a genius to become great without the singleness of purpose and the humility to make the best of his talent. The two Englishmen with much the highest batting average against Australia – the acid and time-honoured test – are Herbert Sutcliffe and Ken Barrington, neither of whom, I think, had the genius of David Gower. Yet against Australia, Sutcliffe's average was 66.85, Barrington's 63.46 and Gower's 44.78, and the bowling that the first two faced was certainly no weaker than when Gower himself was fighting for the Ashes. The disparity is a matter partly of technique, partly of temperament and partly of disposition. In Gower's case, his inborn genius could even have been a handicap, deluding him, at times, into thinking that he could come to no harm.

We can do no more than conjecture how the players of one age would have fared against those of another. They played what may seem a quaint, homespun sort of game a hundred years ago, and a quainter one before that. But how might the modern 'superstar' have coped with the 'fast and ripping round-arm' of Alfred Mynn, on pitches much rougher even than that at Sabina Park in February 1998, when the Test match there was abandoned, or with G.H. Simpson-Hayward's underarm lobs? Not very comfortably, I fancy – anyway to start with.

Simpson-Hayward was a successful bowler during the 'Golden Age' of batsmanship. Having had the Australians (the legendary Victor Trumper was playing) in no little trouble when bowling for Worcestershire against them in 1909, he went to South Africa with the MCC team that winter and took six for 43 in the first innings of the First Test match and 23 wickets in the five-match series. 'In bowling,' said Wisden, 'the real honours were carried off by Simpson-Hayward, who found the matting wickets very much to his liking.' There was, and still is, much to be said for matting wickets.

The game's champions can do no more than be the best of their time. I have seen all the leading cricketers of the last sixty years, and got to know many of them well, and if, in placing those that I have chosen, I was influenced by friendship and affection, it was only very faintly so. I could never have left out Leslie Ames, otherwise. He had been a hero of mine well before I reported on his hundredth first-class 100, scored for Kent against Middlesex on the last day of the Canterbury Week in 1950. Although rising forty-five at the time, and 'gone in the back', he was still dancing down the pitch to the Middlesex spinners as if he was Fred Astaire. A splendid wicket-keeper and brilliant fielder, Ames was everyone's idea of a natural cricketer, and when, after he had finished playing, he managed MCC teams to Pakistan and the West Indies, he did so with the same easy and instinctive touch. He must, I suppose, be one of those 'sins of omission'.

There are another 100 cricketers and 500 after that, who have touched greatness on their day. Between the early 1970s and the early 1990s the standard of fast bowling reached unprecedented heights. Not all of it was particularly edifying, and to an altogether disproportionate degree it dominated the game; but to hold a place as a fast bowler in the West Indian sides captained by Clive Lloyd and Vivian Richards, it was necessary to rank among the best and most fearsome there have ever been. Batsmen who came up against Andy Roberts or Joel Garner or Colin Croft when they were fired up and playing for West Indies will think it a travesty that none of them has found a place in this particular pantheon. If they failed to do so because they bowled too often at the batsman and not enough at the stumps, I make no apologies.

Of less renown, but from all accounts a great fast bowler, was J. Barton King, the American who took England by storm when on tour with the Philadelphians in 1897, 1903 and 1908. As a baseball pitcher, 'Bart' King had studied the theory and practice of swing, and as a bowler he put it to extraordinary and innovative use. I have left out Jeff Thomson, too – Dennis Lillee's redoubtable partner when Australia were winning nine out of their twelve home Test matches against England and West Indies between December 1974 and February 1976. There was an elemental grandeur about Thomson in action, just as there had been about Frank Tyson.

After watching West Indies routed at Adelaide in 1976, I asked Sir Donald Bradman who was the fastest bowler he thought he had ever seen. Having first of all sung the praises of Lillee and Thomson, he plumped not for an Australian or a West Indian but for an Englishman – and it was not, as one might have expected it to be, Harold Larwood. For sheer pace, he put Tyson at the top of his list, bowling as he had under Len Hutton's captaincy at Sydney, Melbourne and Adelaide in 1954–55.

Greatness in cricket does not reside solely in figures, but in manner, in character, in style and in impact; yet still what arouses some may strike no chord in others. To expand upon this, I shall select a few personal favourites, who, to me, were great players as well. When, for example, with bated breath I used to watch Martin Donnelly in the Parks at Oxford just after the Second World War, it would have been unthinkable to leave him out of the best fifty cricketers there could ever have been, let alone the best hundred. Gloucestershire would bring their full side to play the University in those days – more often than not it was their first first-class match of the season – and that meant seeing Walter Hammond, Charlie Barnett and that wise old bird, Tom Goddard. And Goddard rated Donnelly with Bradman as the best batsman he had ever bowled against. New Zealand's batting has never been seen to better advantage than when Donnelly and Bert Sutcliffe, another very fine left-hander, were at the wicket together on their tour of England in 1949.

High among my relatively unsung heroes are Bhagwat Chandrasekhar, the Indian leg-spinner who overcame poliomyelitis to win Test matches in places as far apart as Bombay, Melbourne, Port of Spain and the Kennington Oval, and Johnny Wardle, who could bowl the perfect chinaman, the perfect googly and the perfect left-armer's orthodox spinner in the same over. As a conjuror with the ball, Wardle was scarcely less versatile than Shane Warne.

At around the time that Wardle was settling into the Yorkshire side, Arthur Morris and Sid Barnes were opening the innings for Bradman's 1948 Australians; the very personification, they were, of Australian remorselessness, a truly forbidding pair. When I came to know them I discovered Morris was a man of exceptional charm and gentleness and Barnes an irrepressible joker and the best of fun. If Alec Bedser failed to account for Morris early in an Australian innings, England knew to expect a long score from him.

Built like a pillbox, Barnes had a pulverizing square cut and an insatiable, often mischievous desire to farm the bowling. By the time of my first tour of Australia, with F.R. Brown's side in 1950–51, Barnes was in the press box, writing a cheerfully irreverent column for the Sydney *Daily Telegraph*, entitled 'Like it or Lump it'. 'You put in a black (carbon) for me today, Neville,' he would say to the great Neville Cardus, 'and I'll do the same for you tomorrow. They'll never know the difference.'

I am sad not to have found a place for Tom Graveney, one of the most graceful of all English batsmen and the maker of 122 lovely first-class hundreds, or for the inimitable Patsy Hendren, the maker of 170 such happy hundreds, or for George Gunn, one of the great originals who must have batted, perhaps more than anyone else, like Denis Compton. I burn candles, too, for Roy Marshall and Colin Milburn, both unacclaimed but unforgettable, and I used to marvel at the batting of the younger Nawab of Pataudi. Of these last three, none had a career average higher than 35, yet each one was a great batsman in his way. Greatness is to be found in the eye of the beholder, not only in the pages of Wisden.

Like the triumverate of mighty West Indian Ws – Clyde Walcott, Everton Weekes and Frank Worrell – Marshall was born in Barbados, and when the four of them played in the same Test side, against New Zealand at Auckland in 1952, it was Marshall who was accorded the privilege of going in first wicket down. In terms of talent and as an entertainer he was the equal of the others. Among white West Indians, only George Challenor of a previous generation has been of anything like the same calibre as Marshall.

After he had helped Hampshire to win their first county championship in 1961 I eventually cajoled Marshall into saying how many times he had been well and truly got out that season, as distinct from contributing to his own downfall through his devil-may-care approach to batting. 'Maybe once,' he said, a little self-consciously. The bowler was Ted Dexter, the venue Portsmouth and the ball in question pitched outside Marshall's leg stump and clipped the off bail. 'I can't play those,' he added. It is only because Dexter could bowl such balls as that that I have placed him ahead of Peter May. As a batsman pure and simple, May might just have shaded it.

Colin Milburn was one of the last of the laughing cavaliers. Among the final dozen or so innings he played before losing his left eye in a road accident at the age of twenty-seven were one of 243 for Western Australia against Queensland in the Sheffield Shield at Brisbane, a century for England against Pakistan at Karachi and an unstoppable 158 in the only championship match he played at the start of the 1969 season before being virtually lost to the game. To cricket as a whole, but especially to English cricket, Milburn was a priceless asset, an irreplaceable source of power and light relief. The afternoon session at Brisbane, in which he scored 181 of his 243, is high among those I would most like to have seen.

Pataudi batted as if aware of his rank as much as of his undoubted genius. He, too, had a dreadful car smash but, unlike Milburn's, the horribly damaged eye, in his case the right one, was saved, which left him with the focus that Milburn was denied. Even with such a handicap, Pataudi made a double hundred for India against England in a Test match in Delhi and averaged 56 in a Test series in Australia. After watching him score 75 and 85 against Australia at Melbourne, with a torn hamstring and only one eye and a bit, good judges in Australia were prepared to class him with the very finest. But if fate had not prevented him from achieving the widest recognition, his nonchalance might have.

The two Indian batsmen of recent times featured in these pages are Sunil Gavaskar and Sachin Tendulkar. Pataudi was less idolized than either but every bit as gifted as both. If Australians make the most beligerent cricketers, South Africans the most dedicated, New Zealanders the most earnest and West Indians the most mercurial, those born on the Indian sub-continent can play strokes that would enter the heads of no others. The English, without the sparkle and the confidence begotten by warmth and sunshine, are journeymen by comparison. The fact that they monopolize this book is only because they have played the game for so much longer and in much greater numbers than anyone else. You may be sure that in a generation's time there will be more than six Pakistanis and but a single Sri Lankan in everyone's top 100.

I am not of the view that cricket is endowed with fewer characters than it used to be. It is just that they have become harder to recognize. Perish the thought, but had Alfred Mynn or W.G. or Warwick Armstrong or Jack Hobbs or Denis Compton or Len Hutton batted in a helmet, they would be remembered nothing like as vividly or as visually or as fondly as they are. At all levels the game is being taken more seriously and tackled more vigorously than it was twenty-five years ago. The merest hint of unconformity is likely to be frowned upon.

The manners of cricket reflect society in general. They always have. And that means that the game is becoming increasingly more regimented, ever more materialistic and audibly more aggressive. But still it enriches the moment and gilds the memory, and its roots continue to spread. I am quite sure that those who achieve cricketing greatness today would have done so at any time. Whether their predecessors of long ago would have excelled at the modern game, or would have wanted to, I am not so certain. But that is a sociological question quite as much as a cricketing one.

William Gilbert **Grace**

*'For nearly forty years he bestrode
the sporting world . . .'*

When W.G. Grace died in 1915 at the age of sixty-seven, Lord
Harris, who had captained him in his first Test match in 1880
(the first ever to be played in England), said: 'It is difficult to
believe that a combination so remarkable of health, activity,
power, eye, hand, devotion and opportunity will present itself
again.' Well, it is eighty-three years ago now that W.G. died, and
he remains the most magnificent figure in the history of the game.
For nearly forty years he bestrode the sporting world, his face as
well known as any on this earth.

He was fifteen when he made 32 and 22 for Bristol & District
against an All-England X1, and fifty-eight when he made 74 in
the last of his 151 innings for the Gentlemen against the Players.
In 1895, when rising forty-seven and of megalithic proportions,
he 'renewed all the power of his youth' in becoming the first
batsman ever to score 1,000 first-class runs in May.

Besides his 54,896 runs, he took 2,876 wickets, first at a
briskish round-arm and then with something slower and more
artful, and as a doctor he had a country practice near Bristol to
think about. Sometimes irascible and occasionally domineering,
yet endearingly modest and invariably kind, he was said to have
a distinct distrust of learning.

When asked which of all his innings he recalled with the
greatest satisfaction, he chose one that was not even in a first-
class match. It was the 400 not out he scored in thirteen and a
half hours for a United South of England X1 against 22 of
Grimsby & District at Grimsby in 1876. 'Well,' he said, 'they all
fielded, and they hadn't cut the grass.' Enthusiasm, stamina, pride,
humour and insatiability – that one story embraces them all.

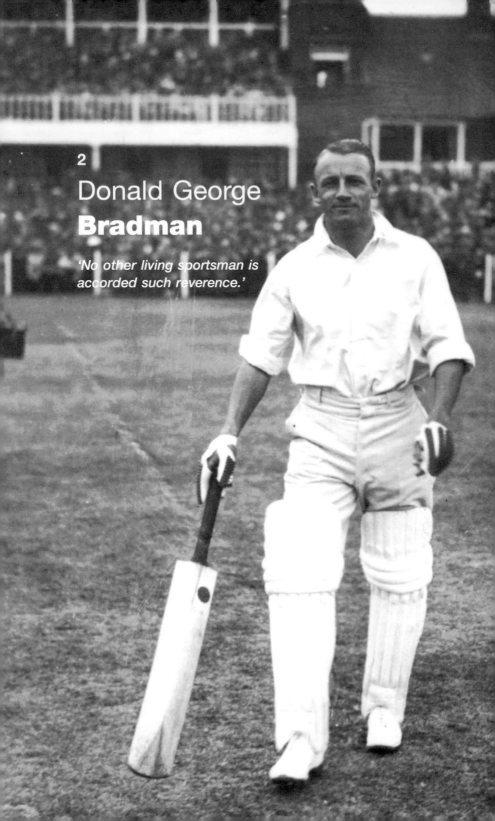

2

Donald George
Bradman

'No other living sportsman is accorded such reverence.'

By their thousands, pilgrims still beat a path to the home in Adelaide of Sir Donald Bradman, the most famous Australian of all. They may not get a glimpse of him, for, having been a very public figure, he is now, at the age of ninety, a very private person; but they will have paid their homage.

No other living sportsman is accorded such reverence. He is more than a legend; he became a demigod because of his extraordinary feats. In 338 first-class innings (W.G. played well over a thousand more) he made 117 hundreds and averaged 95.14; in 52 Test matches he made 29 hundreds and averaged 99.94. In every match in which he played he doubled the attendance and gave his side the equivalent of a hundred-run start; and he had a cricket brain that was second to none. To make a relatively ordinary mortal of him, if only for one series, England devised body-line, a form of bowling lacking in sportsmanship, based on intimidation and involving the use of up to six short legs.

Yet Bradman himself believes there were other players of his time who were potentially just as good. What they may have lacked were the same illimitable reserves of concentration. His eyes, when they were tested in his youth, got an alpha, as it were, rather than the expected alpha double-plus; but he had the mind to achieve greatness, and to have achieved it, had he chosen to, in many other fields. This could be seen from the care and perception which he brought to the game's administration when his playing days were over.

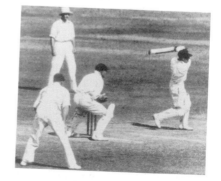

Gary Sobers was everything that could be asked of a cricketer – the complete all-rounder, a supreme sportsman and delightfully modest. Don Bradman believes that there can never have been another such innings played in Australia as Sobers's 254 for the Rest of the World X1 on the Melbourne Cricket Ground in the new year of 1972. He described it as 'one of the historic events of cricket'.

For much of the 1960s Sobers was simultaneously the best batsman in the world, the best left-arm swing bowler, as good an all-round fielder as there was and a spinner who could bowl in the orthodox style or out of the back of the hand, according to need. He laughed a lot, and when stumps were drawn there were no recriminations.

As a captain, Sobers was not especially successful, being too easy-going for one thing and too often preoccupied with his golf swing or the result of the next race for another. Even with the help of his own genius, West Indies won only nine of the thirty-nine Test matches in which he led them. He did, however, have one remarkable series as captain: in England in 1966, when West Indies won three of the five Test matches and lost only one, he scored 722 runs at an average of 103.14, took twenty wickets and held ten catches.

By the time he and a gammy knee had had enough he had scored 8,032 runs for West Indies, taken 235 wickets for them and held 109 catches. From February 1958 until May 1994 his 365 not out for West Indies against Pakistan at Kingston, Jamaica, was Test cricket's highest individual score. It was one of many reasons why he came to be knighted by the Queen on the racecourse in Barbados in February 1975, as fitting a venue for the horse-loving recipient as for the horse-loving monarch herself.

Garfield St Aubrun **Sobers**

'He laughed a lot, and when stumps were drawn there were no recriminations.'

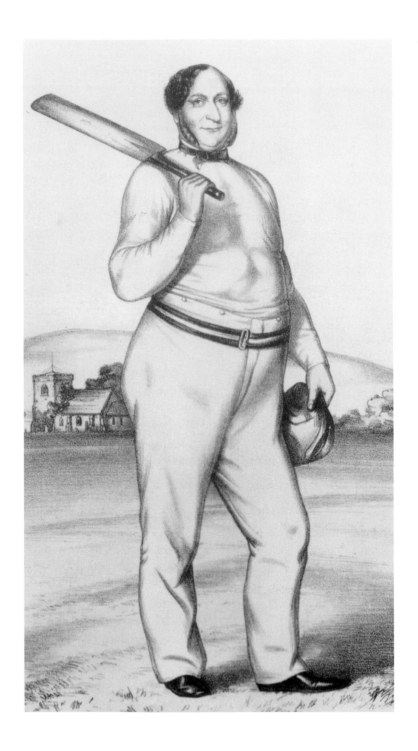

Alfred **Mynn**

'. . . the first and the finest of the "fast and ripping" round-arm bowlers . . .'

The first cricketer to be accorded the title of 'the Champion' was 'kind and manly Alfred Mynn'. For more than a decade he was unbeaten in single-wicket combat. Born at Goudhurst in 1807, the son of a 'gentleman farmer', he was the W.G. of his day.

Mynn was the first and the finest of the 'fast and ripping' round-arm bowlers, as well as a formidably fierce hitter and great catcher of the ball, with 'hands the size of a leg of mutton'. It was said he bowled so fast that he once hit a long-stop such a blow in the chest that he spat blood for a fortnight. On seeing his towering 20-stone figure – 'massive, muscular and tall' – a Frenchman being initiated in the mysteries of the game exclaimed: 'Voila, le grand Mynn.' He would have been wearing a white top hat, a stiff collar and a bow tie.

Soon after Mynn's death in 1861, when W.G. was making a name for himself as a player, a well-wisher presented him with Mynn's pads with the assertion that he alone was worthy of wearing them. H.S. Altham, cricket's most favourite historian, wrote of Mynn that 'only W.G. has ever so completely captured by prowess and personality alike the hearts of his own generation'.

But perhaps his best-known epitaph comes from William Jeffrey Prowse:

All were proud of him, all loved him . . . As the changing seasons pass,
As our champion lies a-sleeping underneath the Kentish grass,
Proudly, sadly will we name him – to forget him were a sin –
Lightly lie the turf upon thee, kind and manly Alfred Mynn.

5

John Berry **Hobbs**

'. . . of his 197 first-class hundreds, ninety-eight were made after his fortieth birthday.'

Never was a cricketer more universally liked and admired than Jack Hobbs. He was liked for his charm and modesty, and admired for his consummate skill as a batsman on every kind of pitch. Between 1905 and 1934 he scored 61,237 runs at an average of 50.65, despite losing five prime years to the Great War. As something of an afterthought, he was knighted in 1953.

Born and brought up in Cambridge, where his father was groundsman at Jesus College, Hobbs played his first first-class match on Easter Monday 1905, for Surrcy against the Gentlemen of England captained by W.G. He scored 18 and 88. After getting 28 and 155 in the next match, against Essex, he was awarded his county cap in instant recognition of a wonderful talent. So sound and enduring was his method that of his 197 first-class hundreds ninety-eight were made after his fortieth birthday. Of his fifteen Test hundreds, twelve were against Australia, nine over there. He scored 3,024 runs at an average of 70.32 in his forty-third year, 2,949 at 77.60 in his forty-fourth and 2,542 at 82.00 in his forty-sixth.

At Melbourne in 1924–25 he and Herbert Sutcliffe batted all through the third day of the Second Test Match. At the Oval eighteen months later and again at Melbourne in 1928–29 the same pair defied inestimable odds on two fiendish pitches to lead England to victories over Australia. And from cover point, where he had no equal, he ran out fifteen batsmen on one Australian tour alone, an average of one a match. To all who knew him and countless thousands who didn't he was known affectionately as 'the Master'.

6

Sydney Francis **Barnes**

*'He was someone with whom no one
took liberties, either on or off the field.'*

As a rule, any debate on the greatest bowler in the history of the
game is soon over: Sydney Francis Barnes is returned *nem. con.*
In a sense this is surprising, for he was not very fast and he was
not very cunning and he played in only twenty-seven Test
Matches; but he was very daunting and very relentless, and, as
Neville Cardus wrote, 'a chill wind of antagonism blew from him
even on the sunniest day'.

Barnes had only two full seasons of first-class cricket – in
1902 and 1903, both for Lancashire. By playing, instead, for
Staffordshire and in the Staffordshire League he felt he remained
fresher, and it was made financially worth his while. He was
someone with whom no one took liberties, either on or off the
field. He played when he wanted and said what he liked. P.F.
Warner did not take him to Australia in 1903–04, with the first
MCC side, because of his moods.

But when England did turn to him it was never without
advantage. His Test career began in Australia in 1901–02 after
A.C. Maclaren, who was due to take an England side there, had
come up against him in a net at Old Trafford. Until then Barnes
had played only one first-class match; but in his first two Tests
alone, at Sydney and Melbourne, he took nineteen wickets.

Erect and unfailingly accurate, with a full follow-through, he
gripped the ball firmly between his first and third fingers, with
the palm of his hand facing the batsman, and spun it fiercely
either way, enough to draw blood towards the end of a long spell.
The last 49 of his 189 Test wickets came in only four Test matches
in South Africa in 1913–14. To batsmen, his bowling on the mat
out there was a living nightmare.

7

Walter Reginald **Hammond**

*'English batsmanship was seen then
at its very finest.'*

All who played with Walter Hammond in the fifteen years before
the Second World War were in awe of his ability. He scored, all
told, 50,511 first-class runs at an average of 56.10, took 732
wickets at medium-pace without much enjoying bowling and
held 819 catches, most of them at slip. Of his 167 hundreds, 36
were of 200 or more, and yet many were the days when he simply
couldn't be bothered.

The word most often used to describe his cricket was
'majestic'. One of the greatest of all sporting pictures shows
Hammond driving through the covers, the blue silk handkerchief
which he always carried, fluttering from his right trouser pocket.
For poise, balance, grace and power it is cricket *in excelsis*. Off
the field, too, there was a proconsular air about him, so that
when at the age of thirty-five he became an amateur, having
played as a professional until then, it seemed only right and
proper.

Yet his early years were not all plain sailing. He missed a
season through having to qualify for Gloucestershire and another
when he was gravely ill following a tour of the West Indies, and
his first fourteen Test innings failed to produce a century. The
next five – all in Australia in 1928–29 – were 251, 200, 32 (run
out), 119 and 177. There were days when Bill O'Reilly, the great
Australian wrist spinner, found a way of shackling him by
bowling at his legs to an on-side field. But O'Reilly was in the
Australian side when Hammond made 251 not out at Sydney in
1936–37 and again when he made 240 in the Lord's Test of 1938.
English batsmanship was seen then at its very finest.

8

Isaac Vivian Alexander
Richards

*'. . . he had a swagger of which no one
could be oblivious.'*

Others have made more runs at a higher average, but the most
daunting figure to have walked through a pavilion gate in modern
times with a bat under his arm must be Vivian Richards. In the
right mood he was a magnificent, irresistible player. It is unimag-
inable that anyone has ever hit the ball harder or with more
thrilling strokes.

Brought from Antigua to Somerset in 1973, when he was
twenty-one, all he lacked was discretion. Already he thought no
bowler was good enough to tie him down, and against England
in England in 1976 he was right: in seven innings in that series
he scored 829 runs at an average of 118.42. He was strong,
muscular, confident, handsome, athletic, sensitive and fiery, and
he had a swagger of which no one could be oblivious.

He was also ambitious, not so much for himself as for Afro-
Caribbeans in general, and when the time came for him to lead
West Indies he was ruthless in the way he exploited his fast
bowlers. He was, in fact, made to wait longer for the captaincy
than he wanted, and he was relieved of it, after six years, when
he was still keen to take West Indies into the 1992 World Cup.

He had become more masterful than was wise by then, but,
for all his tempestuousness, he was a wonderful cricketer. The
only semblance of a question mark concerned his own form
against a string of very fast West Indian bowlers. In the hotbed
of Bridgetown, when playing there for the Leewards or the
Combined Islands against Barbados, he was seldom his most
dominant self. With 8,540 Test runs, at an average of 50.23, he
heads the West Indian list – with Brian Lara still 4,000 runs
behind him.

Because there were times when he was wayward and others when he could be wanton, not everyone would count Ian Botham among the ten best cricketers there have ever been. It is true, too, that against the West Indian sides of the 1980s he made no great impact, partly through trying to play them at their own game. But against England's other opponents, particularly Australia, he was a towering figure with an incomparable record.

In Test cricket he scored fourteen hundreds, took 383 wickets and held 120 catches, some of unimagin-able brilliance. He took only twenty-one Test matches to reach 1,000 runs and 100 wickets, twenty-seven fewer than Garfield Sobers and nine fewer than Imran Khan. His achievements in the Third, Fourth and Fifth Test Matches against Australia in 1981 were nothing short of sensational. In two of them – at Headingley and Old Trafford – he was the reincarnation of Gilbert Jessop; in the other, in a desperately tight finish at Edgbaston, he took Australia's last five wickets in twenty-eight balls for one run.

He took the whole country with him; he was not only his captain Michael Brearley's great match-winner; he was his prompter too. As a captain himself, Botham lacked the necessary gravitas; but he was a giant of a cricketer none the less. His generosity as an opponent is mirrored in his work for charity, if not always in his views on those who run the game.

9

Ian Terence **Botham**

'As a captain, Botham lacked the necessary gravitas; but he was a giant of a cricketer none the less.'

Denis Charles Scott
Compton

'He danced to his own bewitching tune . . .'

To have a true picture of the unique charm with which Denis Compton batted at his best, it is necessary to be over fifty. This is because no one has played like him since, and there is very little vintage Compton on film that is readily available.

He was game for anything. Most of all he liked to go down the pitch when the bowler was running in, both as a technical and psychological ploy. He was always improvising, usually by instinct and often in someone else's shirt and with someone else's bat because he had left his own behind. He danced to his own bewitching tune, and, there being no helmets in those days, everything showed – the enjoyment, the looks that attracted a film star's fan-mail and the little asides.

Compton scored 38,942 never boring, often magical, runs at an average of 51.85, 3,816 of them, including eighteen hundreds, in 1947, the golden summer of balmy days and longed-for peace. He had not only all the strokes in the book but countless others that he made up as he went along. In between times he took 622 wickets with miscellaneous left-arm spin, again doing what came naturally, and in the winter, before a battered knee half-crippled him, he played on the wing for the Arsenal, his career in football ending when he hobbled up the steps at Wembley in 1950 to collect his FA Cup-winner's medal. Such virtuosity is not possible today, though until the day he died (St George's Day, 1997) 'Compo' liked to think it would be.

11

Leonard **Hutton**

'. . . his knighthood, bestowed in 1956 in gratitude for The Ashes, was lightly worn.'

From the moment that he broke the world record Test score by making 364 for England against Australia at the Oval in 1938, when he was only twenty-two, Len Hutton's name has been written in gold. He had a natural, polished style, endless patience, self-effacing charm, a laconic sense of humour, a sumptuous cover drive and a sure eye for the main chance. His mentor was Herbert Sutcliffe, his first regular opening partner for Yorkshire. 'He's a marvel,' said Sutcliffe of his young protegé in 1934, 'the discovery of a generation.'

An accident with a vaulting horse during the Second World War, while on a physical training course in York, left Hutton with a visibly shortened left arm and his admirers with fears for his cricketing future. That he still became the mainstay of England's post-war batting and went on to lead them, as their first professional captain of the twentieth century, to two famous Ashes victories, and to finish with an average of 56.46 against Australia, was proof of the man as well as the player.

He was as resourceful on difficult pitches as he was reliable on good ones. But he was never physically robust, and the strain of it all took a lot out of him, particularly on his last, triumphant tour of Australia in 1954–55. A crushing defeat in the First Test at Brisbane was a fearful blow, and the next three Tests, though all won, were so fraught that before the second of them he was near to breaking point. His record of 40,140 runs (average 55.75) and 129 hundreds speaks for itself; his knighthood, bestowed in 1956 in gratitude for the Ashes, was lightly worn.

Frank Edward **Woolley**

'. . . the regal splendour of his cricket . . .'

Between 1906 and 1938 Frank Woolley scored 58,969 runs, took 2,068 wickets, held 1,095 catches and came to be known as the Pride of Kent. It is worth reading those figures again, for they will never be repeated.

But it was for the regal splendour of his cricket and his Olympian detachment that Woolley is remembered even more than for his remarkable record. He was not only very tall, he was straight-backed as well, so that literally as well as metaphorically he looked down upon his fellow men. He never walked to the wicket without a buzz of anticipation, nor seemed hurried when he got there. With a defence that was based on attack, he gave many a Kent innings a flying start. He bowled orthodox left-arm spin from a great height and very accurately, and when fielding at slip, which is what he mostly did, he had the advantage of a telescopic reach.

Even today when a left-hander plays a particularly elegant cover drive, as David Gower used to do, there are cries of 'Woolley'. Yet for such a marvellous all-rounder his Test record was a little disappointing. He won the first of his sixty-four England caps in 1909 and the last in 1934 when, at the age of forty-seven, he was controversially and deferentially but unsuccessfully brought back to go in first wicket down against Australia in the last Test at the Oval. Of happier memory are his 95 and 93 against the all-conquering Australians in the Lord's Test of 1921, two magnificent innings in a lost cause.

Shane Keith **Warne**

*'. . . Warne appeared, purveying the most
beautiful and bewildering assortment of leg-breaks,
top-spinners, googlies and flippers.'*

All being well, Shane Warne will go on enthralling us for some years yet. Aged twenty-nine he is still young for a spinner; but were he never to bowl another ball, his light would continue to shine, so salutary has been his effect on the game.

At a time when Test cricket was falling ever more deeply under the influence of the fast-bowling juggernauts, Warne appeared, purveying the most beautiful and bewildering assortment of leg-breaks, top-spinners, googlies and flippers. It was wonderful, other than for the batsmen who had the job of unravelling him. The fact that he was fair-haired, bushy-tailed, blue-eyed and attractive to the young made it all the better.

Perhaps the three most talked-about balls ever bowled were the one from Ernest Jones that went through W.G.'s beard at Sheffield Park in 1896, the bumper from Harold Larwood that hit Bill Woodfull above the heart at Adelaide on the body-line tour, and the first ball Warne bowled against England, which was at Old Trafford in 1993 and pitched outside Mike Gatting's leg stump and removed his off bail. Already Warne has over 300 Test wickets to his credit – and he is still four years younger than Clarrie Grimmett was when he bowled his first leg-breaks and googlies for Australia and only a year older than Bill O'Reilly when he did.

14

Barry Anderson
Richards

'. . . not so much batting as divine inspiration.'

When he put his mind to it, Barry Richards could give the perfect exhibition of batsmanship – elegant, orthodox, versatile and powerful. At times, though, his mastery bored him and the bowlers were spared.

In a sense he was a genetic freak, there being no real trace of sporting achievement in his family. His misfortune was to be blossoming at the time of South Africa's removal from international competition. He had played only four Test matches, in which he averaged 72.57, when they were expelled in 1970. But for this, he would surely have been a mainstay of what had all the makings of a great South African side.

Richards had to be content, instead, with county cricket for Hampshire, Sheffield Shield cricket for South Australia, Currie Cup cricket for Natal and counterfeit cricket for Kerry Packer. His greatest masterpiece was an innings of 356 for South Australia against Western Australia at Perth in 1970, described at the time as being not so much batting as divine inspiration. Having married an Australian girl, he became an administrator for the South Australian Cricket Association, then for the Queensland Cricket Association, and came to regret, upon reflection, that he had not cashed in more often when he had had the bowlers at his mercy.

Victor Thomas **Trumper**

*'His generosity, like everything else
about him, was beyond words.'*

'As modest as he was magnificent,' was Sir Pelham Warner's
assessment of Victor Trumper. 'A beloved and legendary hero,'
was how Bill O'Reilly, the great Australian bowler, put it. 'I felt
like a boy who had killed a dove,' lamented Arthur Mailey after
playing against him for the first time in Sydney and bowling him
out with a googly.

Of Trumper the batsman, C.B. Fry said: 'He had no style
and yet he was all style.' He dealt with good length balls in the
way that others dealt with half-volleys and long-hops. To many
who saw them both play, Trumper was more brilliant even than
Bradman, albeit vastly less prolific. On only one of his four tours
of England was he consistently successful. That was in 1902, a
very wet summer in which he made eleven hundreds.

Of his eight Test hundreds the finest came on that tour of
1902 when, on a soft pitch, he made 104 before lunch on the
first day at Old Trafford, having been enjoined by Joe Darling,
his captain, when he went in to 'take good care'. The highest of
the eight was his 185 against England at Sydney the next year.
At his sports shop in Sydney a few days later, a young customer
asked him whether it might be possible to buy a bat which
Trumper himself had used. 'You can have this one if it's any
good to you,' Trumper replied. 'It's second-hand because I played
with it against England the other day. They cost twenty-five bob
new, so you can have it for ten.' His generosity, like everything
else about him, was beyond words. He died of Bright's Disease
when only thirty-seven, and the cricket world went into
mourning.

Imran **Khan**

'He knew what he wanted and went for it . . .'

For as long as he wanted to be, Imran Khan was the prince of Pakistan cricket, and he played the part to perfection. When he gave the game his full attention he was a great all-rounder.

Under his captaincy, Pakistan could be expected to play to something like their true ability: some would say that this was his defining achievement. It was after he had led them to the World Cup in Australia and New Zealand in 1992 that he retired to do other things, most particularly to build a cancer hospital in Lahore. He had taken 362 Test wickets by then (only Kapil Dev, Richard Hadlee, Malcolm Marshall and Ian Botham have ever taken more), sometimes bowling at a fierce pace, scored six Test hundreds and kept the company of some of the world's most beautiful women. That two of his Test hundreds were made from number six in the order, three from number seven and one from number eight gives an idea of how many more he might have made had he batted higher up.

Even in his Oxford days, Imran had a disdainful air: it was the Pathan in him. He knew what he wanted and went for it, and he talked intelligently about cricket, though not always objectively about the standard of English umpiring. There have been very few more prodigious bowling feats than his forty wickets at an average of 13.95 in the Test series between India and Pakistan in Pakistan in 1982–83. As an aspiring politician he has yet to find the same irresistible length.

Keith Ross **Miller**

'. . . the sort of cricketer we would all like to be . . .'

There was never a more popular or spontaneous sportsman than Keith Miller, who first came to public attention in the Victory Tests in 1945, when he strode to the wicket almost straight from the cockpit of his night-fighter aircraft. He was the sort of cricketer we would all like to be, and he did his best to let us share in the incarnation.

He was named Keith Ross after Sir Keith Scott and Sir Ross Smith, who had just made the first flight from England to Australia together when he was christened, and England has long been his second home. It was in one of those Victory matches that Miller announced himself by making 185 in 165 minutes, one of his seven sixes scaling the very heights of the Lord's pavilion. He was just as likely to bowl a bouncer off a four-yard run-up as a googly off a full one. If he was not wondering what had won the last race he could catch brilliantly at slip; he could play long and boring innings, if he chose, as well as exhilarating ones; he enjoyed defying convention; he was a magnificent athlete and a great sportsman, and all his life he has kept his countless friendships in good repair, much to the benefit of the Australian telephone service. For many years seldom a day has passed when he has not been on the line to some friend or other around the world.

His bowling partnership with Ray Lindwall, and his jousting with Don Bradman, his first Test captain, were renowned, as was the sight of him top-hatted in the Royal Enclosure at Ascot. If anyone dared to bowl him a bouncer he could look ruffled, but it was unlikely to happen a second time, the threat of retaliation being the deterrent that it is.

Richie **Benaud**

'Dedication was his guiding principle.'

No cricketer ever had a shrewder, more calculating eye for the main chance, or even for the half chance, than Richie Benaud. It made him an outstanding captain when he was already a fine, accurate, probing wrist-spinner, a splendid attacking batsman and an absolutely top-class fielder.

Dedication was his guiding principle. In South Africa in 1957–58 he spent long hours in the nets developing his bowling, spurred on, rather than carried away, by the exceptional all-round success he was already enjoying in the middle. When, very soon, he was given the Australian captaincy, he left nothing to chance and gave nothing away, either outwardly or tactically. He could just as well have captained Australia at poker. The psychology of the job appealed to him, and he got away to a flying start by regaining the Ashes in Australia in 1958–59 from an England side that had been expected to retain them.

Australia's memorable series with West Indies, which began with the tied Test match at Brisbane, came next, for which the two captains, Benaud and Frank Worrell, shared much of the credit, and later that year (1961) Benaud, the bowler, had his own greatest triumph when he plucked the brand (in this case the Ashes) from the burning by going round the wicket at Old Trafford and destroying a burgeoning England innings. By then he was, as he has remained ever since, one of the game's best-informed observers and more august commentators.

19

Dennis Keith **Lillee**

*'Lillee had the resolutely independent streak
of many fast bowlers, only more so.'*

Australia's most redoubtable fast bowler of the nineteenth century was F.R. Spofforth, 'the Demon', who took ninety-four wickets in eighteen Test matches between 1871 and 1887. His reincarnation a hundred years later, not least in appearance, was Dennis Lillee, who took 355 wickets in seventy Test matches between 1971 and 1984 and would have had many more but for a stress fracture of the back and making common cause for a couple of years with Kerry Packer, the Australian entrepreneur.

Lillee had the resolutely independent streak of many fast bowlers, only more so. If he was requested not to practise in short trousers at Lord's, the chances were that he would wear them. He was a magnificent bowler, an irrepressible exhibitionist, an impenitent bully and a great student of the theory and practice of bowling, which enabled him to be wonderfully effective to the day he retired from Test cricket at the age of thirty-four.

No touring side ever got a much nastier shock than MCC's to Australia in 1974–75. They knew nothing of Jeff Thomson, except that he had played one singularly unsuccessful Test match against Pakistan two years earlier, and expected to find a convalescent Lillee. Instead, these two swept all before them. Not even Ray Lindwall and Keith Miller or Brian Statham and Frank Tyson or Wesley Hall and Charlie Griffith or Michael Holding and Andy Roberts made a more formidable pair of opening bowlers than Lillee and Thomson against England in Australia in 1974–75 and against West Indies in Australia the following season. In retirement, from Manchester to Madras, Lillee has been a fine and enthusiastic bowling coach.

Alec Victor **Bedser**

'. . . no day was too long for him, no sun too hot.'

Over the years, Alec Bedser has become as much an institution as a legend. His knighthood in the New Year honours of 1997 was for what he stands for as much as for what he had done on the cricket field. His bowling was a reflection of the man: it was strong, big-hearted and uncompromising.

In successive series against Australia in 1950–51 and 1953 he took sixty-nine wickets at 16.87 apiece. Don Bradman thought the leg-cutter with which Bedser knocked back his off stump on an Adelaide feather-bed in 1946–47 was as good a ball as he ever received. Happily, it was the start of a close and lasting friendship.

At a full medium-pace and with the benefit of hands the size of baseball gloves, Bedser spun the ball as much as cut it, and if he bowled a long-hop it rated a mention on that evening's news bulletin. He had a classical action, and no day was too long for him, no sun too hot.

His playing days over, he helped to choose many England sides and he managed others, always with infinite concern. More recently, a familiar sight at the Oval has been Bedser and the former prime minister, John Major, talking cricket. Never far away is Alec's twin, Eric, the older only by the time it takes them to tell you that things are not what they were, and himself a good enough all-rounder, as a workmanlike batsman and off-spin bowler, to be given a Test trial in 1950.

George Alphonso **Headley**

'. . . in his shorter Test career Headley came nearer than anyone to being as dashingly prolific a batsman as "the Don".'

It was with good cause that George Headley came to be known as the 'black Bradman', he and the great Australian having much in common. They were of a similar size; only nine months separated them in age and in his shorter Test career Headley came nearer than anyone to being as dashingly prolific a batsman as 'the Don'.

With very little coaching behind him, Headley played for Jamaica against Lionel Tennyson's MCC team in 1928 when he was not yet twenty, making 71 and 211. Two years later, in his first Test match for West Indies, he made 21 and 176 against England at Bridgetown, followed by 114 and 112 in the third Test of the same series and 10 and 223 in the fourth. He made two hundreds in his only Test series in Australia, in 1930–31, and in the Lord's Test of 1939 he made 106 out of 272 in West Indies' first innings and 107 out of 225 in their second.

When, with war threatening in August 1939, West Indies were obliged to abandon their tour of England while they could still get a sailing home, Headley had made ten hundreds in nineteen Test matches and was averaging 66.72. By the time West Indies played Test cricket again he was getting on for forty and the eye upon which he had relied so much was nothing like as sharp as it had been. Of the three great West Indian 'Ws', the one who most resembled Headley in physique and style was the equally indomitable Everton Weekes.

Raymond Russell **Lindwall**

*'. . . many a cricket lover's idea of heaven was
the sight of Lindwall bowling to Hutton . . .'*

Ray Lindwall was a beautiful bowler and an endearing man,
whose partnership with Keith Miller, both on and off the field,
held the sporting world in thrall after the Second World War.
They had everything – style, menace, youth and looks.

Nothing could subvert Lindwall's love for the game or his
natural ability to swing the ball in both directions and often
bewilderingly late. Len Hutton rated him the finest bowler he
faced, and in those post-war years many a cricket lover's idea of
heaven was the sight of Lindwall bowling to Hutton, at Lord's
or Sydney according to taste, with Denis Compton padded up to
come in next.

Lindwall's genius lay in his rhythm, his greatness in his virtuosity, his charm in his geniality. The extent to which he dragged
his back foot in the delivery stride, a
propensity of fast bowlers and leg-spinners, could be said to have contributed
towards the focal point of the no-ball law
being switched from the back foot to the
front, and as an attacking force the years
diminished him sooner than was to be
the case with Dennis Lillee, the next
truly great Australian fast bowler.

But the game throws up few such
treasures as Lindwall. Of no more
than medium height, he could bat as
well as bowl (Test hundreds against
both England and West Indies testify
to that), and from all accounts he could have played any
type of football for a living. Having spared the time to smell the
flowers while he was playing, he became a florist when he retired.

Sunil Manohar **Gavaskar**

'. . . a batting method that relied less upon eye and more upon the textbook than that of most Indians.'

Sunil Gavaskar's game was based on an astute mind, a privileged youth and a batting method which relied less upon eye and more upon the textbook than that of most Indians. In spite of the occasional unaccountable rush of blood early in an innings, he made thirty-four Test hundreds, seven more than anyone else ever has, and scored 10,122 runs for India at an average of 51.12. Of his hundreds, thirteen were against West Indies, seven of them in the Caribbean, and eight against Australia.

He was in the line of small, squarely-built Indian batsmen. His brother-in-law, Gundappa Viswanath, was another, and Sachin Tendulkar may yet become the most prolific of them all. Gavaskar had played only six first-class games when chosen to go with India to the West Indies in 1970–71. The sequel was astonishing: in four Test matches there he made 774 runs at an average of 151.80. His first eight innings in Test cricket were 65, 67 not out, 116, 64 not out, 1, 117 not out, 124 and 220, and he was only twenty-one. By comparison Don Bradman's were a relatively modest 18, 1, 79, 112, 40, 58, 123 and 37 not out.

In his 214th and last Test innings, sixteen years later, Gavaskar made 96 against Pakistan, much the highest score of a low-scoring match played on a crumbling pitch at Bangalore. By then he had come to be respected as much for the way in which he handled fame as fast bowling. His commentaries on radio and television are scarcely less deft.

24

Edward Ralph **Dexter**

'. . . a truly majestic hitter of a ball.'

In style and countenance Ted Dexter was the most handsome cricketer of his day. He was a truly majestic hitter of a ball, be it at cricket, golf or rackets, with a presence that was strong in a silent, independent kind of way.

If his 70 in seventy-three balls in the Lord's Test against West Indies in 1963, when he put Wes Hall and Charlie Griffith to flight, is the innings by which he is best remembered, there were many others of equal splendour. He honoured his opponents and yet bludgeoned them. They, for their part, were often in awe of him. After a round of golf in Adelaide one afternoon, Gary Player, who was there to play in the Australian Open Championship, described Dexter as among the best and longest strikers of a golf ball he had ever seen.

Dexter was enamoured with the theory of batting; he could bowl the unplayable ball and catch the uncatchable catch. He attracted comparison with the great Walter Hammond, and, like Hammond, he was not the easiest of communicators when first raised to the England captaincy. In Australia in 1962–63 he seemed at times to treat even his manager, the mighty 16th Duke of Norfolk, like the under-gardener. Not that His Grace would have minded, even if he had noticed. Dexter's retirement, when he was only thirty and as good as he had ever been, was a real deprivation. Among Englishmen, only Ian Botham has since driven the ball with such power or so aroused the Australians.

25

Sachin Ramesh
Tendulkar

'. . . the prodigy of prodigies.'

At Perth in Western Australia early in 1992 Sachin Tendulker made a century for India against Australia on a lively pitch with a brilliance that no other batsman in the world could have surpassed. He was eighteen at the time – the prodigy of prodigies.

In 1997 at Cape Town, by then a veteran of twenty-three and his country's captain, he played an innings of 169 against South Africa that began in a crisis and lasted for five and a half hours and was virtually flawless. In other words, Tendulkar has all the credentials to become one of the two or three greatest batsmen in the game's history, as well as one of the most engaging.

There is no one playing today who would make a better model for a young cricketer to follow, either technically or in terms of attitude. He has a method based on showing the bowler the full face of the bat, and yet the eye to play exotically when he chooses, and he has an instinctive feel for the strategic possibilities of a situation. But only time will tell for how long he is able to withstand the pressures of being India's leading batsman, the relentless idolatry that goes with it, and the worry of wondering, when he is captain and India are on tour, where their next wicket is going to come from.

Besides being a great leg-spin bowler, Bill O'Reilly was one of cricket's most august and stimulating characters. He was a big man with a big heart and big opinions. Born in the bush in New South Wales, he was twenty-six before being taken into the State side. Until then there had been some doubt that an outsize schoolmaster, so physically uncoordinated and with a galumphing run-up and an awkward action could really be the bowler his figures in Sydney Grade cricket kept suggesting.

With the Second World War more or less ending his international career when he was thirty-three, O'Reilly had only seven years at the very top. This was long enough, though, for him to take 144 wickets in only twenty-seven Tests and to convince Don Bradman that he was the best bowler he ever played against.

O'Reilly's pace was appreciably quicker than the normal leg-spinner's, and he rolled his leg-break as distinct from spinning it. But he was miraculously accurate and had a wicked googly, which was not only very difficult to spot but bounced as well. He was a fair but fierce opponent, and later, as a journalist, became a fearless critic. When, even in Australia, leg-spinners were threatened with extinction, 'Tiger' O'Reilly was their doughtiest champion.

26

William Joseph **O'Reilly**

'He was a fair but fierce opponent...'

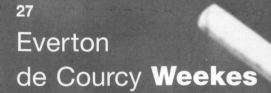

27

Everton
de Courcy **Weekes**

*'... given half a chance, he was down
the pitch in a trice ...'*

Being small, Everton Weekes was essentially a back-foot player, and a brilliant one at that. He was a great hooker and cutter, and given half a chance he was down the pitch in a trice when the spinners came on, sometimes even before they did. Given the forenames of Everton de Courcy, much must have been expected of him, and he let no one down.

His Test batting average of 58.61 is second only to George Headley's (60.83) among West Indians. He is the only man to have scored five successive Test hundreds, which he did against England and India in 1948 and 1949; he was run out for 90 in Madras when on the verge of making it six. Against England at Trent Bridge in 1950, the series in which West Indies finally broke their bonds, Weekes and Frank Worrell added 283 in 210 minutes. Hereabouts, the two most scintillating batsmen in the world were Weekes and the Australian, Neil Harvey, with Martin Donnelly of New Zealand hard on their heels.

Weekes was strong in a stocky way, and he seldom spared the ball. He had such tenacity and courage that after making 90 with a broken finger and on a treacherous pitch against England at Lord's in 1957, Ronnie Aird, then Secretary of MCC, sent him a hand-written note of appreciation on the members' behalf.

There have been a dozen or more Test cricketers who have also played international football of one kind or another – but Weekes alone has won a second 'cap' for bridge. His knighthood in 1995, a KCMG, came for 'services to cricket and public service in Barbados'.

28

Brian Charles **Lara**

*'His problem has been in coming
to terms with his fame...'*

If Brian Lara does not come to be regarded as one of the greatest batsmen of all time, it will not be for want of natural talent. No one ever had more of that. But he has yet to show that he has the mind and the modesty to accommodate it.

At his best he is outrageously brilliant. He plays strokes that are surreal. Attempted by other batsmen, even those of the highest class, they could only end in disaster. He throws the bat at balls of impeccable length and sends them racing through the narrowest of gaps. He holds cricket's two most coveted individual records – the highest first-class score (501 not out for Warwickshire against Durham at Edgbaston) and the highest Test score (375 for West Indies against England in Antigua) – having acquired them, in 1994, within eight weeks of each other.

His problem has been in coming to terms with his fame and not being deflected by his fortune. For someone so idolized and indulged in his youth, this has been much more a test of character than playing breathtaking strokes. Garfield Sobers managed it as if by instinct, but few are born as bounteous as he. Lara is of a more defiant and calculating nature. If the captaincy of West Indies, which he now has, should soften that, and take him out of himself, he will have *Wisden* at his mercy. Chiefly, perhaps, it is a question of humility – for without that no batsman ever quite fulfils his potential.

29

Richard John **Hadlee**

'. . . tall, rangy and sufficiently athletic . . .'

Although he had the advantage of being born into a cricketing family, Richard Hadlee became the great fast bowler that he was only by dint of hard work and strength of character, and by shrewdly pacing himself. His father, Walter, is one of the grand old men of New Zealand cricket; but Walter was a batsman, never a bowler.

Richard was tall, rangy and sufficiently athletic. He was committed to setting himself targets, and in doing so he became an even better bowler than had been anticipated. In Dennis Lillee he had a near-contemporary across the Tasman Sea by whom to judge his own standards, and he suffered nothing by comparison, either in accuracy or renown.

Until Kapil Dev just struggled past him, Hadlee's 431 Test wickets, taken at an average of five a match, was the world record. The longer Hadlee went on the craftier he grew, the more inquisitorial and versatile a bowler he became, so that he was feared more when he was thirty-five than when he had been twenty-five, which is very rare for a fast bowler.

In six Test matches in Australia, when in his middle thirties, he took fifty-three wickets at 13.96 apiece – quite stunning figures. The only period in their seventy-odd years in Test cricket when New Zealand have been a match for everyone was when Hadlee was in his pomp and Martin Crowe was showing the rest of the side how to bat. In 1990 Hadlee became his country's first cricketing knight.

30

Robert Graeme **Pollock**

'. . . his footwork was peculiarly his own.'

Gifted with a wonderful eye and marvellous timing, Graeme Pollock made batting look impossibly easy, even when playing as a boy among men.

At sixteen he became the youngest player to have made a hundred in South Africa's Currie Cup, and in Australia in 1963–64, when still only nineteen, he scored 122 at Sydney and 175 at Adelaide in only his third and fourth Test matches. A year later his 125 made out of 160 at Trent Bridge paved the way for South Africa's first series win in England for thirty years and ranks among the classics. The last of his seven Test hundreds, his 274 against Australia at Durban in 1969–70, was also the largest: it is, in fact, the highest individual score ever made in a Test match in South Africa.

When taken out of circulation by South Africa's expulsion in 1970, Pollock was averaging 60.97 in Test matches and still approaching his prime. Sir Donald Bradman was among his many admirers. 'If ever you play like that again, I hope I am there to see it,' Bradman had said to him at Perth, after watching him make 127 in 108 minutes at the start of his only tour of Australia.

Tall, left-handed and laid back, Pollock played strokes which defied convention, partly because his footwork was peculiarly his own. He and his Test-playing fast-bowling brother, Peter, who took 116 wickets for South Africa, were the sons of the editor of Port Elizabeth's main morning newspaper, himself a former Currie Cup player. With Peter's son, Shaun, now a considerable Test all-rounder, quite a dynasty is developing. But however much it grows, there is most unlikely ever to be another Pollock as exceptional as Graeme.

31

Arthur **Shrewsbury**

*'Even in the nets, he defended his wicket
as though his very life depended on it.'*

To be picked out by W.G. as the best English batsman with whom
he had played secured for ever Arthur Shrewsbury's place in
the hall of fame. On turning pitches, which were in the majority
in those days, he was considered to be superior even to the
Champion himself.

Although never robust, Shrewsbury undertook four long and
arduous tours of Australia between 1881 and 1888, staying on
after the last of them to look after the interests of an English
football team whose visit he had been instrumental in setting
up. He and his fellow professionals, Alfred Shaw and James
Lillywhite, were pioneers in the way in which, helped by spon-
sorship, they took the game to 'the colonies', as Australia was
called then. Of the seven Tests in which Shrewsbury captained
England in Australia, five were won. The next professional
captain to have the chance to win a series there was Len Hutton,
sixty-six years later.

For the last quarter of the nineteenth century W.G. and
Shrewsbury were the pillars of their respective sides in the great
match between Gentlemen and Players, and Shrewsbury held
most of the early records in Tests against Australia. His hundred
at Sydney in 1884–85 was the first ever made by an England
captain; his 164 at Lord's in 1886 was the highest individual score
against Australia until W.G. beat it soon afterwards, and he was
the first to make 1,000 Test runs. Reserved, earnest and well
respected, he had a defence, based on back-foot play, that was
second to none, and his patience was untiring. Even in the nets,
he defended his wicket as though his very life depended on it.

32

Frederick Robert **Spofforth**

'Tall, sinewy and saturnine . . .'

Because he was known as 'the Demon', the name of F.R. Spofforth conjures up visions of the fastest bowler on earth. But it was when he slowed his pace to something nearer fast-medium, with only the occasional very fast ball, that he became the great champion that he was. He might not altogether have escaped the censure of umpires and referees today, for he minced no words; but Australian cricket never had a more inspirational figure.

In just two matches, both in England, Spofforth did more than anyone to establish his country's cricketing reputation. The first was at Lord's in 1878, when, to everyone's amazement, the Australians beat a very strong MCC side in a single day, bowling them out for 33 and 19, with Spofforth taking ten wickets for twenty runs. In the second, at the Oval in 1882, Australia beat England by seven runs and Spofforth was chaired off the field after taking fourteen for ninety in the match. It was after this that the obituary appeared in the *Sporting Times* which began: 'In affectionate memory of English cricket. . . .' – the genesis of The Ashes.

Tall, sinewy and saturnine, with long, whirling arms, Spofforth was a master at varying his pace. His contemporary, George Giffen, said how he '*looked* the Demon, every inch of him'. After playing the last of his eighteen Test matches he settled in England, playing occasionally for Derbyshire, marrying a Lyttelton and making a fortune in the tea business.

33

Peter Barker Howard **May**

*'. . . a retiring disposition and the most renowned
on-drive of the last fifty years.'*

Peter May had a retiring disposition and the most renowned on-drive of the last fifty years. No matter who it was he had just hammered for four, he showed never a semblance of side. He took a lot of knowing, yet he was a player's player.

In his early days, as if by destiny, everything went his way. He made a century in his first Test match while still up at Cambridge, and became, at twenty-five, one of England's youngest captains, with some very fine bowlers (Brian Statham, Fred Trueman, Jim Laker, Tony Lock, Frank Tyson, Johnny Wardle among others) at his disposal. At Sydney and Melbourne in 1954–55 he had Australia's fielders wringing their hands from the force of his strokes, and in 1956 in England he led an Ashes-winning side. As a batsman he was venerated by his contemporaries; as a captain he made himself scarce off the field, but his players were well aware of a decidedly cussed streak on it.

They little knew, though, how much his dual role as England's captain and premier batsman was affecting his health and enjoyment. The press, too, took their toll, and in 1961, when still only thirty-one, he decided he had had enough. It was a profound disappointment, though after retiring he applied himself with equal rigour to cricket administration, both for Surrey and as an England selector. In any such debate, it is almost always Peter May who wins most votes as England's finest batsman since the Second World War.

34

Wilfred **Rhodes**

'. . . an innate cricketing intelligence.'

Over a career which lasted for more than thirty years, Wilfred Rhodes scored 39,802 runs and took 4,187 wickets with flighted orthodox left-arm spin. Having batted at number ten or eleven for his first nine Test matches, he became, within a few years, Jack Hobbs's regular opening partner, putting on 323 with him against Australia at Melbourne in 1911–12, which is still the record partnership for England's first wicket.

Like George Hirst, his Yorkshire contemporary, Rhodes had an innate cricketing intelligence. 'Who is the greatest all-rounder in the world?' Yorkshiremen would ask. 'Nobody knows for sure,' would come the reply, 'but he bowls left-handed and bats right-handed and was born in Kirkheaton.' For that is what both Hirst and Rhodes did, and where they both came from. Rhodes was the more subtle, complex character, and he had to work harder at his game. Yet in 1898, his first season with Yorkshire, he took 154 wickets for them. 'He never gave you a long-hop,' said Johnny Tyldesley, 'you had to go looking for one.'

In Australia in 1903–04 he took thirty-one wickets at 15.74, the best figures ever returned there by an Englishman of his type; in 1911–12, by when he was going in first rather than ninth or tenth, he averaged 57.87 with the bat and took no wickets at all. When recalled to the colours at the age of forty-eight, to play against Australia in the last Test match in 1926, he took six for seventy-nine, so helping England to regain the Ashes. Even after he had lost his sight, as he did in old age, he could have bowled a length, he had got into such a way of it.

MOONSHINE'S CRICKETERS.—MR. K. S. RANJITSINHJI.

35

Kumar Shri **Ranjitsinhji**

'. . . playing as no one else had
ever been seen to do.'

Colonel His Highness Shri Sir Ranjitsinhji Vibhaji, Maharaj Kumar Jam Sahib of Nawanagar, better known as K.S. Ranjitsinhji or 'Ranji', was the first great oriental batsman. He burst on the scene in the middle 1890s, having been neglected as a cricketer for the first three of his four years at Cambridge.

He was of much the same shape and size as Mohammed Azharuddin of the present Indian side, anyway in his playing days, being quite tall, very supple and with a game which consisted of strokes that 'looked like conjuring tricks'. Being an 'original', and playing as no one else had ever been seen to do, he became, in England, an immediate sensation.

Taking Sussex to his heart, Ranji brought to that county some of their best years. By 1900 he had twice scored 3,000 runs in an English season, something which not even W.G. had done. As Neville Cardus put it: 'He expressed not only his own genius but the genius of his race.' He made 62 and 154 not out in his first Test match, for England against Australia at Old Trafford in 1896 (another thirty-six years were to pass before India were to play Test cricket), and 175 in his first Test match in Australia, at Sydney in 1897–98. In the English winters, when he was not on tour, he either stayed in England for the shooting (he lost an eye in the shooting field) or took a ship to India, there to live a princely life and to succeed, eventually, to the throne of Nawanagar.

36

Allan Robert
Border

*'The longer he played
the tougher he got . . .'*

Even after playing 156 Test matches for Australia, 153 of them in succession, and captaining them 93 times, and scoring 11,174 runs in 265 Test innings, and taking 156 catches – these are all records by a long way – Allan Border wanted more. It was only with the utmost reluctance that he accepted his redundancy, although by then he was in his fortieth year.

More than anything, it was his tenacity that kept him going. The longer he played the tougher he got, in spite of having to contend with some of the shortest, fastest bowling ever seen – from the West Indian sides of the 1980s.

As a result of not being recruited by Kerry Packer for his World Series Circus, Border was playing Test cricket earlier than he otherwise would have been. In time, this gave him the seniority to inherit the Australian captaincy, a job which he was not born to do and didn't care for at first, but which he gradually grew into.

His sheer doggedness pulled him through two or three chastening years, and for this he was rewarded in his last twenty-nine Tests with the services of Shane Warne, one of history's greatest match-winners. Border, left-handed and short of inches, became one of Australia's sporting icons, a status usually reserved for racehorses or highwaymen.

Frank Mortimer Maglinne
Worrell

'On and off the field Worrell had style.'

Between August 1924 and January 1926, within little more than a mile of each other in Barbados (an island barely larger than the Isle of Wight), were born the three great West Indian 'Ws' – Clyde Walcott, Everton Weekes and Frank Worrell. There was a knighthood to come for each one of them, first to Worrell in 1964 for what he had brought to the game.

On and off the field Worrell had style. He played the most effortless strokes, and when he became the first regular black captain of West Indies he exerted an equally effortless authority. He seemed to take everything in his elegant stride. But he could be perverse, too – as when he batted with exaggerated caution for eleven hours twenty minutes while making 197 not out against England at Bridgetown in 1959–60.

In his first seven Tests against England, three in West Indies and four in England, he scored 833 runs at an average of 104.12 without breaking sweat. Although a right-handed batsman, he bowled left-arm, at medium pace with the new ball and slow orthodox spin with the old. But perhaps it was as captain of West Indies on their great tour of Australia in 1960–61, which ended with him and his side being given a ticker-tape farewell from Melbourne, that he was seen at his most impressive. Having died, sadly early, of leukaemia, he was accorded a Memorial Service in Westminster Abbey.

Clyde Leopold **Walcott**

'. . . actively involved with the first-class game, mostly at the highest level, for fifty-five years.'

When Clyde Walcott stepped down as Chairman of the International Cricket Council in 1997 he had been actively involved with the first-class game, mostly at the highest level, for fifty-five years. The first day of his first first-class match – 17 January 1942 – was his sixteenth birthday.

Of the three great West Indian 'Ws', Frank Worrell was the most lissom and languid and Everton Weekes the shortest and sturdiest. Walcott was the biggest and broadest batsman of his day. The unbroken partnership of 574 between the young Walcott and the young Worrell for Barbados against Trinidad in 1945–46, which is still only three runs short of the highest in the history of the game, must have brought a classic contrast in styles. With his eye in, Walcott was a terrific hitter of the ball, especially through the covers. But he was much more than that.

No one has ever matched his record between March 1953 and June 1955 when he made ten pounding hundreds in twelve successive Test matches – two against India, three against England and five in a losing series against a very strong Australian attack in the Caribbean. He had given up wicket-keeping by then, a job to which he was never physically suited, and was bowling well enough at medium-pace to claim the wickets in Test cricket of Len Hutton, Tom Graveney, Willie Watson, Richie Benaud, Neil Harvey and Keith Miller. From 1993 until 1997, as cricket's equivalent of Secretary General to the United Nations, Walcott was a firm yet conciliatory administrator, held on all sides in some awe. His knighthood, for services to the game, came on Barbados's Independence Day in 1993.

39

William **Beldham**

'He was everyone's first pick.'

Known as 'Silver Billy' because of his fair hair, blue eyes and rosy cheeks, William Beldham played his first game for Hambledon, the great Hampshire cricketing cradle, in 1787, when he was twenty-one. His last first-class appearance was for Godalming in 1821. He lived to be ninety-six and to see even more changes in the game than someone who was born in 1902 and is still alive today.

For much of his career, Beldham was the finest batsman in England. He was everyone's first pick. Like Denis Compton a century and a half later, he startled bowlers by jumping out to meet them – by 'giving them the rush' as it was called then – and like Compton, too, he was at his best at Lord's. He was a superb cutter of the ball: 'Here', wrote the Reverend John Mitford, 'he stood with no man beside him, the laurel was all his own. His wrists seeme to turn on springs of finest steel.' To level up the first Gentlemen and Players match in 1806 he was 'given' to the Gentlemen, who, having won by an innings, stood after that on their own feet.

Beldham played before the round-arm revolution, bowling slow under-arm, the ball delivered high from under the arm-pit, curving in the air, turning either way and generating bounce off the pitch. He was also an outstanding fielder. A picture of him in his smock hangs in the Long Room at Lord's today, quite holding its own with those of other great players on the adjoining walls.

40

George Alfred **Lohmann**

*'. . . more tanned and handsome
than was altogether good for him.'*

Owing to ill health (he died in South Africa of tuber-
culosis when he was only thirty-six) George Lohmann
had a sadly short career, albeit a glorious one. His rise
was meteoric. Within two seasons of joining the Surrey
staff in 1884, he was taking twelve Australian wickets
in a Test match on his home ground and spearheading
an English victory.

He was a completely natural cricketer with a
superb physique, though more tanned and handsome
than was altogether good for him, or so some thought.
Although he was no more than medium-fast he had
a repertoire that kept the batsmen guessing. 'Owing
to his naturally high delivery the ball described a
pronounced curve and dropped rather sooner than the
batsman expected. . . . He was the perfect master of
the whole art of varying his pace,' wrote C.B. Fry.
Lohmann had spin and cut as well as flight, and the
heart to bowl all day.

The amount of work he undertook may have
hastened his end. In only 186 matches for Surrey he
took 1,458 wickets, a striking rate of very nearly eight
a match. Even for England his striking rate of 6.2 a
match has been bettered only by S.F. Barnes. In his
first three Tests in Australia, all at Sydney in 1886–87,
Lohmann took twenty-five wickets for 189 runs. And
he could bat too, when he put his mind to it. It sounds
very much as though George Lohmann was the Ian
Botham of his day.

41

George **Hirst**

'. . . this "Agamemnon of Yorkshire".'

In the annals of English county cricket there has never been an *annus mirabilis* to compare with George Hirst's in 1906. In that one season he scored 2,385 runs and took 208 wickets; he reached the double of 1,000 runs and 100 wickets after only sixteen matches, in one of which, for Yorkshire against Somerset at Bath, he made 111 and 117 not out, took 6 for 70 and 5 for 45, and caught no less a warhorse than Captain H.S. Poyntz.

A left-arm bowler and right-handed batsman, this 'Agamemnon of Yorkshire' owed his success with the ball to length and swing. But it was only when he cut down his run and reduced his pace that he became consistently effective. No other county but Yorkshire has ever had as contemporaries two such prolific all-rounders as Hirst and Wilfred Rhodes. Although Rhodes was six years the younger, they played together over 400 times in the same Yorkshire side.

As a batsman capable of adapting his game to the needs of the moment, Hirst made sixty centuries: his 341 against Leicestershire at Leicester in 1905 remains the highest individual score ever made for Yorkshire. In comparison, his Test record was somewhat disappointing, partly because at that level he lacked the pace to trouble the best Australian batsmen on good pitches. For eighteen years after he had finished, he coached the boys at Eton with pride and affection.

Herbert **Sutcliffe**

'. . . there was never a hair out of place.'

Herbert Sutcliffe's claim to greatness has the surest of foundations – a batting average of 66.85 for England against Australia, built up over twenty-seven matches and forty-six innings. It is he, too, rather than Len Hutton or Geoffrey Boycott, who monopolizes Yorkshire's batting records.

A 'made' as distinct from a 'natural' player, Sutcliffe constructed for himself a well-nigh foolproof technique to augment an imperturbable temperament. It brought him 50,138 first-class runs (average 51.95), including 149 hundreds. The English summer of 1931 was memorably wet and the pitches were uncovered; yet Sutcliffe still scored 3,006 runs at an average of 96.96. At the wicket, nothing seemed to rattle him, nor was there ever a hair out of place. If he was disconcerted by the behaviour of a ball or the enmity of a bowler, he never betrayed it. On rain-affected pitches his skill was legendary, and in Jack Hobbs for England and Percy Holmes for Yorkshire he found two ideal opening partners.

When an England innings was in the hands of Hobbs and Sutcliffe all seemed well with the world. They opened together in twenty-five Test matches, in fourteen of which England's score was past 100, in one innings or both, before a wicket fell. Their *average* partnership going in first for England was 88.

Offered the captaincy of Yorkshire as a professional in 1927, an almost unthinkable departure in those days, Sutcliffe declined it. In such matters as that, too, he had sound judgement.

Michael John **Procter**

*'. . . a robust all-rounder of rare
ability and great appeal.'*

Mike Procter was another victim of South Africa's years in the wilderness. He was not yet twenty-four and had played only seven Test matches for them when they were expelled. In these he took forty-one wickets at 15.02 apiece, made red-blooded runs and looked what he was – a robust all-rounder of rare ability and great appeal.

So he took up with Gloucestershire, and became one of the very best and most popular overseas signings any English county has ever made. There was never a more wholehearted cricketer. He so threw himself into the affairs of Gloucestershire, both on and off the field, that there were times when they found themselves being called Proctershire.

On his day Procter was as fast a bowler as any in the world, despite appearing to deliver the ball off the wrong foot, a peculiarity which, if anything, amplified his in-swing. All his Test appearances came in two home series against Australia, and a very nasty shock it was that Bobby Simpson's side got when this young blond bombshell, only just out of his teens, came hurtling in at them at Durban early in 1967, making the ball fly round their ears.

He was as natural and dashing a batsman as any in the game (in 1970–71 he hit six successive hundreds for Rhodesia in the Currie Cup) and a splendid fielder. Ian Botham had nothing on him, apart from the chance to play ninety-five more Test matches.

44

Gregory Stephen **Chappell**

*'. . . a poised and natural stylist, possessed
of a strongly independent streak.'*

Perhaps once in a decade, the members of MCC rise in unison in
the pavilion at Lord's to acclaim a Test innings. Greg Chappell's
131 in 1972 was saluted in this way, mostly for its beauty and technical merit, though it also helped to end Australia's run of eleven
successive Test matches without a victory over England.

The grandsons of Victor Richardson, who took the Australian
side to South Africa in 1935–36, the three Chappell brothers –
Ian, Greg and Trevor – were a mixed and talented lot. If nepot-
ism played some part in Trevor's cricket career, it certainly didn't
with Ian, an inspirational captain of Australia and a real street-
fighter at the crease, or with Greg, a poised and natural stylist,
possessed of a strongly independent streak. One of the most
talked-about strokes of the last fifty years was Greg Chappell's
on-drive. It was to be compared with Peter May's.

Greg Chappell's Test career began when he was twenty-two,
with the first of his twenty-four Test hundreds. Coming in against
England at Perth, in something of a crisis, he cruised, as if by
right, to 108. He finished, thirteen years later, with a batting
average of 53.86, which only Don Bradman has ever bettered for
Australia. Chappell was also a magnificent all-round fielder – a
brilliant swooper in the covers and as safe as anyone when in the
slips to Dennis Lillee and Jeff Thomson. His ratio of 122 catches
in 87 Tests bears testimony to that.

Of the thirty-two bowlers to have taken more than 200 Test wickets, only two (Waqar Younis and Malcolm Marshall) have had a faster striking rate than Fred Trueman. On average he took a wicket with every forty-nine balls he bowled. By way of comparison, Dennis Lillee took one every fifty-two balls, Ian Botham one every fifty-six balls, Jim Laker one every sixty-two balls and Kapil Dev one every sixty-three balls. Waqar's average is a freakish forty-three; Marshall's was forty-six. Shane Warne's is sixty-four.

Trueman was England's first counter to Australia's Ray Lindwall after the Second World War – a fast bowler of superb rhythm, timing and diversity. He was also one of the great characters and raconteurs of the game, whose occasional reluctance to conform cost him a lot more dearly in terms of selection than it would today.

Because of it, he missed out on tours to both Australia and South Africa when he was at his best. Yet he still became the first bowler to take 300 Test wickets, and his aggregate of 2,304 first-class wickets is the highest ever achieved by a fast bowler. Although he played a few Sunday League matches for Derbyshire in the twilight of his career, no Yorkshireman has been more susceptible than Trueman to his native county's declining fortunes. In retirement, too, he has become renowned as a *laudator temporis acti*. His microphone manner is one of pained and measured dismay as England suffer another of their less glorious days. 'I just dawn't oonderstand it' is an oft-heard lamentation.

Frederick
Sewards
Trueman

*'... the first bowler to
take 300 Test wickets ...'*

Tom **Richardson**

'. . . magnanimity and wholeheartedness.'

For a fast bowler, Tom Richardson had a remarkable record. In a short career and without ever having the benefit of a second new ball, he took 2,104 wickets, 1,074 of them in only four years in the 1890s. Most of them were for Surrey, but he was successful in Test cricket too, both in England and Australia.

He may be said to rank among the immortals, not only because of his great skill and strength and the fact that he was such a fine sight in action, but for his magnanimity and wholeheartedness. 'Bad luck, sir,' he'd say when he took the wicket of someone who was not very good, 'it was the best ball I've bowled all summer.' When asked whether he thought the number of balls in an over should be increased from five (which it generally was until 1900) to six, he said: 'Give me ten.'

In the Old Trafford Test match against Australia in 1896 he gave a wonderful exhibition of resourcefulness and stamina. Having taken seven for 168 in sixty-eight overs in Australia's first innings and seen England follow on against 'a majority of 181', as Wisden put it, he all but brought Australia down when they went in again, needing only 125 to win. Bowling unchanged for three hours, Richardson took another six for seventy-six in 42.3 overs. Described by C.B. Fry as being a 'cheerful brown-faced Italian-looking brigand with an ivory smile', he bowled a full length and possessed a break-back from the off that was as famous at the Oval as Alec Bedser's leg-cutter fifty years later.

47

Michael Colin **Cowdrey**

'. . . seldom, if ever, seen to hurry his stroke.'

When Ernest Cowdrey gave his only son the initials
M.C.C., in the hope that one day he might be some
good at cricket, he could have been tempting providence. But providence came to the party, and for
more than fifty years Colin Cowdrey has been
lending distinction to the game.

By the time he was thirteen he was making 73
and 44 and taking eight wickets with some parabolic
leg-breaks for Tonbridge against Clifton at Lord's,
and in all the 188 innings he went on to play for
England he was seldom, if ever, seen to hurry his
stroke. Allied to this natural aptitude were a sound
and trusted method, a cover drive renowned for its
elegance, a love of the game which has been proof
against permanent disenchantment, and a modesty
and sense of humour which have withstood the test
of fame. Nothing – not 22 Test hundreds, nor 42,719
first-class runs, nor 107 first-class hundreds, nor the
record fourth-wicket partnership in Test cricket of
411 with Peter May, nor the Presidency of MCC,
nor the Chairmanship of the Cricket Council, nor a
knighthood, nor even a peerage has turned his head.

At his best he was like a galleon in full sail. He
was also a brilliant slip-fielder and a great ambas-
sador. All he lacked to make him not only the
despair of bowlers, which his defence ensured, but
their constant scourge as well, was a pinch of daring.
It was sometimes said of him that he alone didn't
know just how good he was.

48

Kapil **Dev**

'at some stage or other Kapil galvanized
most games in which he played . . .'

Without playing at all like the traditional Indian cricketer, Kapil Dev became their foremost all-rounder, with a world record haul of 434 Test wickets to his credit. Having been born in the bracing foothills of the Himalayas, he had the physique to play as very few Indians ever have. He bowled not with spin and patience but at a good strong pace, and with a bat in his hand he was not so much deft as bold and dashing.

Of his 131 Test matches, the majority were played in the 1980s, when Ian Botham, Richard Hadlee and Imran Khan were also in their prime, and Kapil withstood the inevitable comparisons. Besides all those Test wickets, he also scored eight Test hundreds, all great fun to watch.

He saved some of his most expansive performances for Lord's. It was in the Test match there in 1982 that, on one and the same evening, he made a blazing 89 in fifty-five balls and took England's first three wickets in his own first four overs; and it was at Lord's again, in 1990, when India had nine wickets down and still needed twenty-one to save the follow-on, that he straight drove four successive balls from Eddie Hemmings, the England off-spinner, to the Nursery End for six. How the members blinked! But at some stage or other Kapil galvanized most games in which he played, either with his enthusiasm or independence or bravado or power.

49

Hugh Joseph **Tayfield**

*'. . . his front foot dug a hole where
no one else's ever had.'*

The wiliest exponents of flight in the second half of the present
century have been the two Indians, Bishen Bedi and Erapally
Prasanna, and the South African off-spinner, Hughie Tayfield.
Tayfield was a ritualist, too.

Before every over he bowled, he kissed the springbok badge
on his cap; before every ball, he tapped his toes on the ground
(hence the nick-name 'Toey'); he had a run-up of no more than
three or four yards, and bowled so close to the stumps that his
front foot dug a hole where no one else's ever had – six inches
in front of the middle stump of the bowler's wicket. Even the
field he used was unusual, with two very straight, quite deep
forward short-legs, and no mid-on. He had confidence, cunning
and supreme control.

In the 1950s, he tormented and then trapped the finest
batsmen of England and Australia. There were days when Denis
Compton, Neil Harvey, Peter May and Keith Miller all raged at
their inability to hit him out of the attack. At Johannesburg in
1956–57, in the second of the Test matches to be played there
on that tour, England, needing only 232 to clinch the series, had
reached 147 for two on the last afternoon, with Colin Cowdrey
and Doug Insole playing well and Peter May and Denis Compton
still to come. But it was Tayfield who was being carried shoulder-
high off the ground soon after tea. He had, to boot, the allure
of a matinée idol and attracted the following of one, which no
doubt had something to do with his being married five times.

50

Bishen Singh **Bedi**

'. . . all ease and hidden danger . . .'

Bishen Bedi, the slow left-armer from northern India, must rank among the most spell-binding bowlers of this century. Coming in off a short, beguiling run, in a pink or sky-blue turban, he had a lovely action, all ease and hidden danger, and as much spin as he needed, coupled with those little variations of line and length and loop and swerve which keep the batsman wondering and deflect monotony.

He could be watched for hours on end without the day dragging, and if he had the off-spinner from southern India, Erapally Prasanna, as his partner, so much the better. The game of cricket needs good Indian spin bowling; it is one of its most precious assets, and there is no country in the world where it cannot be successful.

Of Bedi's 266 Test wickets, 35 were taken in England, 35 in only seven matches in Australia and 33 in nine in the West Indies. He alone among Indians has ever taken 1,000 first-class wickets. He took 1,560 all told, 434 of them for Northamptonshire. On the field he had the patience and temperament and stamina of an artist; off it he had his differences with authority, especially in India, although as often as not he had common sense on his side, as well as an abiding love of the game.

At the age of twenty-one, Neil Harvey had already made five hundreds for Australia and had a Test average of 120. Such youthful brilliance has never been surpassed, even by W.G., Don Bradman, Garfield Sobers, Javed Miandad or Sachin Tendulkar.

Left-handed and the smallest member of most of the sides in which he played, Harvey was unsurpassed as a player of spin. 'The ball can't turn if it doesn't bounce,' he used to say, and he had the twinkling footwork to put this precept into practice. He began as a fledgling under Bradman's wing, and when, in time, Richie Benaud was preferred to him as Australia's captain, Harvey became his most loyal lieutenant.

To enjoy his cricket, Harvey had to play it adventurously. This was part of his charm as well as of his menace as an opponent. One of his most remarkable innings, though – the undefeated 151 with which, on a turning pitch, he won the Durban Test match against South Africa in 1949–50 – was a miracle of vigilance. Only Bradman, Allan Border and Greg Chappell have scored more Test hundreds for Australia than Harvey, and no one can have fielded any better. First in the covers, from where he had a right-arm return, and then at slip, by when he had to wear glasses, he was wonderfully good. Of his five brothers, three also played first-class cricket, one, Mervyn, for Australia.

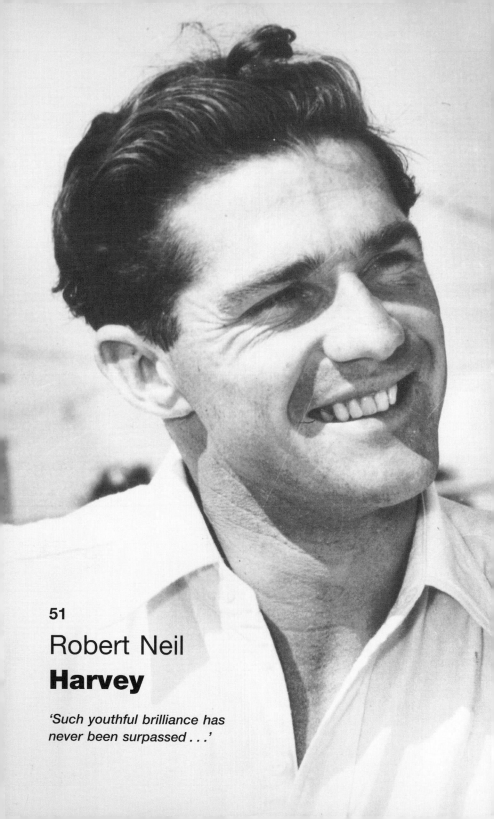

51

Robert Neil
Harvey

*'Such youthful brilliance has
never been surpassed . . .'*

52

Rohan Babulal **Kanhai**

'His cricket was all about self-expression . . .'

Such was Rohan Kanhai's genius for batting that, had he been so minded, he might well have averaged not 47 in Test matches for West Indies but 77 or even 87. But he would not then have been the great attraction that he was.

His cricket was all about self-expression, a good deal more so at times than was in the best interests of his side. When the urge took him, he would suddenly swing himself off his feet and fall spread-eagled across his crease in an attempt to cart the ball out of the ground. No batsman ever got himself out more than Kanhai, as distinct from being got out.

In terms of pure talent he was in Don Bradman's class, and of much the same stamp – slight, eagle-eyed and incredibly quick-footed. When he applied himself he was a wonderful player on every sort of pitch. No one ever played the ball later or had more strokes. When Kanhai and Gary Sobers were in together for West Indies it was just as exciting as when Everton Weekes and Frank Worrell had been, and even more a celebration of Caribbean abandon.

In the first three of his seventy-nine Test matches Kanhai, the tyro, kept wicket, against England in England; in his last thirteen he was West Indies' captain. Deciding one day in 1974 that he had nothing better to do, he helped John Jameson add 465 for Warwickshire's second wicket against Glamorgen at Edgbaston, one of the half-dozen highest partnerships in the history of the county championship.

53

Charles Burgess **Fry**

'. . . had something of the appearance
of a Greek god.'

As a sportsman-cum-scholar, C.B. Fry was, and still
is, second to none, and it was cricket's good fortune
that for nearly twenty years he gave the game a
large part of his time. He was not a natural batsman
so much as a severely and brilliantly analytical one,
and he had something of the appearance of a Greek
god.

His sporting honours were as memorable as
they were multifarious. He held the world long-
jump record (23ft 6½ins) for twenty-one years,
played soccer for England and rugger for the
Barbarians, and scored 30,886 first-class runs at an
average of 50.22. 'In cricket, triumph and disaster
will come again; but, in this world, Charles Fry will
not,' said R.C. Robertson-Glasgow, a scholar and
writer of like style.

As a batsman Fry was in his prime around the
turn of the century. In 1901, when he scored 3,147
runs at an average of 78.67, his last six innings were
all centuries. When he went to the crease next, at
the end of April 1902, for London County against
Surrey at the Oval, he made 82, having played for
Southampton in the FA Cup final two days earlier.

He once said of his batting: 'I really only had
one stroke, but it went to ten different parts of the
field.' It was played off the front foot, mostly with
the bottom hand, and was a form of applied
science. As a conversationalist he had, as it were, a
multitude of strokes, and was ever ready to air
them – to those who could keep up.

Graham Gooch was arguably the best player of genuinely fast bowling England have ever had. For someone who was not especially quick on his feet, his success against the fearsome West Indian attacks of the 1980s and early 1990s was heroic.

It was achieved not so much by getting behind the line of the ball, a dangerously overrated practice, as by getting alongside it and so giving himself room to play as he chose. Although a batsman of high promise as a young man, he was some time maturing, but he made up for that by remaining until well into his forties a marvellously consistent run-maker. Had he not announced his retirement from Test cricket at the end of an unlucky tour of Australia in 1994–95, he could have played another dozen times for England.

A surprising appointment and some-what reluctant appointee as England's captain when David Gower was eased aside at the end of 1989, Gooch led them thirty-four times, averaging very nearly 60 in the process and making something of a fetish of personal fitness. It was as England's captain against West Indies at Headingley in the First Test of 1991 that he played his finest innings: without a shadow of doubt his 154 not out, when he carried his bat through England's second innings, won a low-scoring match for his side. His 118 Test appearances, 8,900 Test runs (despite having started his Test career with a 'pair' against Australia in 1975) and scores of 333 and 123 in the same Lord's Test match against India in 1990 are but three of his many records. Tactically, he was rather more pedestrian.

Graham Alan
Gooch

'. . . until well into his forties, a marvellously consistent run-maker.'

Alan Philip Eric **Knott**

'. . . a jack-in-the-box and a splendidly competitive cricketer.'

As a brilliant wicket-keeper and the maker of five Test hundreds, Alan Knott rates among the best all-rounders England have ever had. Jack Blackham, Bert Oldfield and Don Tallon were three great Australian 'keepers; Godfrey Evans, Herbert Strudwick and Bob Taylor were other Englishmen in a comparable class behind the stumps; but none of these had Knott's batting skills.

He was Mr Punch, and an acrobat, and a jack-in-the-box and a splendidly competitive cricketer. Strange though it may seem, he started life as a bowler who batted, and even when he first went for trials with Kent he was advised to concentrate on his bowling. That was until Leslie Ames, himself in the line of great Kent wicket-keepers and more renowned as a batsman than Knott, saw him behind the stumps.

Knott was still only twenty-one when he got into the England side. That is exceptionally young for a wicket-keeper; but he was such a perfectionist, and kept himself so fit and immaculately groomed, and batted with such nimble ingenuity and became such a thorn in the side of the Australians that he was an automatic choice for England until he went off to play for Kerry Packer and then to South Africa when they were in balk. He finished with 269 Test victims, and is to be seen now, complete with video camera and binoculars and Thermos flask and sandwiches and the same bony little figure, scouring the country for wicket-keepers on behalf of the England selectors.

56

Alan Keith **Davidson**

*'Although a big man, he was
a smooth and powerful mover.'*

Batting in the lower middle-order for Australia, and opening the bowling and fielding anywhere, Alan Davidson was an even more explosive all-rounder than his redoubtable contemporary, Richie Benaud. Watching Davidson, it was easy to get the impression that, had he so wished, he could have become an Olympic athlete or an international rugby player. Although a big man, he was a smooth and powerful mover.

He did everything left-handed, which included bowling very fast late in-swingers with the new ball. Even Davidson himself, let alone the batsman, was surprised sometimes by the way the ball swung and in which direction. Bowling from over the wicket, he kept the slips in constant expectation with the ball slanting across or cutting away from the right-handed batsman. Some of the world's best players were leg-before to him, shouldering arms when they expected the ball to go the other way.

He was a marvellous catcher, and with a full swing of the bat he could hit the ball vast distances. When he felt like it, he could also make the slightest of niggles look to all the world like a multiple fracture. In South Africa in 1957–58 his colleagues bought him his own massage table, a folding one that could travel with him. Since finishing as a player, he has established a reputation as a discursive and diligent host at the Sydney Cricket Ground, where he has been, for these many years, President of the New South Wales Cricket Association.

Kenneth Frank
Barrington

*'As coach to the England side, he was
a father to some, a brother to others
and a friend to them all . . .'*

If it were possible to draft any one England batsman
of the last thirty-five years into an England side for
an Ashes series, just to show what is meant by the
bulldog spirit, Ken Barrington would be a natural
choice. When he stuck out that jaw of his, the
Australian bowlers knew what they were in for: in
thirty-nine innings against them he averaged 63.96,
seven more than Len Hutton and sixteen more than
Geoffrey Boycott.

Many were the tears that were shed when, at the
age of fifty, Barrington died from a heart attack
during a Test match in Barbados in March 1981. As
coach to the England side at the time, he was a father
to some, a brother to others and a friend to them
all; he endured their travails as if they were his own.

He was a tremendous natural cricketer, though
many of his strokes he cut out in pursuing the path
he chose for himself, that of an insatiable, not to say
obsessive, accumulator. He could field anywhere and
bowled good enough leg-breaks and googlies to
account for Gary Sobers (twice) and Clyde Walcott
among several distinguished Test victims. On faster,
bouncier pitches than England's he might well have
become a considerable all-rounder. Of his twenty
Test hundreds four were reached with a six. These
came, as a rule, over wide long-on and ended a long
period of gruelling self-denial.

Javed **Miandad**

'. . . a genius as a batsman and as an improviser.'

With 8,832 runs and twenty-three hundreds in 124 Test matches at an average of 52.57, Javed Miandad is Pakistan's most prolific batsman, and they are unlikely ever to have one who is more tenacious. He was so good that he worked out his own way of playing, one that was very bottom-handed and depended on instinct and a marvellous eye at least as much as on the text-book.

He loved a good set-to. Niggling the opposition was a favourite pastime, and at times he went too far with it, as when he and Dennis Lillee squared up to each other in a Test match at Perth. Miandad courted controversy. But he was a genius as a batsman and as an improviser. His first five Test innings, against New Zealand in Pakistan in 1976–77, were 163, 25 not out, 25, 206 and 85; against India at Hyderabad in 1982–83 (Hyderabad in Sind, that is, rather than southern India) he and Mudassar Nazar shared in a partnership of 451, the fourth highest in Test cricket, Miandad's contribution being an unbeaten 280.

The captaincy of Pakistan was something which he always coveted but was always losing. Against Australia in 1979–80, when he was twenty-two, he became the third youngest Test captain of any country – after the younger Nawab of Pataudi of India and the Australian, Ian Craig. After that he was in and out of office even more often than Benazir Bhutto was as his country's Prime Minister. It was a career that had many glorious moments, but all too little quiet content.

59

Ian Michael **Chappell**

*'. . . turned a struggling team into an
awesomely effective one.'*

As Australia's captain from 1971 until 1975, Ian
Chappell ran his side as though it was an SAS
battery. A great fighter, he turned a struggling
team into an awesomely effective one. Having
lost three of his first five Tests as captain, all
against England (which made the pain all the
worse), he was beaten only twice more in the
remaining twenty-five.

He was as contemptuous of compromise as
he was allergic to ambivalence, and, so long as
they were sufficiently unfastidious, his players
loved him for it. The sight of a crouching, confident, green-capped crescent of Australian slip
fielders, consisting of Ian and Greg Chappell, Ian
Redpath and Doug Walters, with Rod Marsh
behind the wicket and Ashley Mallett in the
gully, as Jeff Thomson or Dennis Lillee ran into
bowl, was enough to strike fear into the hearts
of England's supporters, let alone their batsmen,
and Ian Chappell knew it.

He was a 'dinkum' Aussie – honest, loyal,
blunt, chauvinistic and a very good, if outwardly
rather twitchy, batsman – less elegant than his
brother, Greg, but of equal weight. He came out
of retirement to become one of Kerry Packer's
most prominent endorsers, since when, as a
commentator, he has read the game as astutely
as when he was playing it – and with the necessary expurgations.

60

Wasim **Akram**

*'. . . bowls and bats left-handed with
absolute spontaneity.'*

When the Indian sub-continent was partitioned in 1947, that part
of it where fast bowlers come from – Punjab and the approaches
to the north-west frontier – was allotted to Pakistan. One of
the region's typically strapping specimens is Wasim Akram, a
wonderfully natural cricketer, who bowls and bats left-handed
with absolute spontaneity.

That he was not chosen for Pakistan's tour to South Africa
early in 1998, when he would have been first pick for most other
Test-playing countries, was incomprehensible, even to those
familiar with the consuming instability of Pakistan cricket. Off a
run-up that varies according to his fancy, and with a beautifully
fluent action, Wasim can be a lethal swinger of the ball, and to
conserve his energy he has become a shrewd adjuster of his pace.
Garfield Sobers and the Australian, Alan Davidson, are the only
left-handed all-rounders to have been remotely as dynamic.

Wasim was eighteen when he played his first Test series,
against New Zealand in New Zealand, having been spotted a few
weeks earlier by Javed Miandad, who was casting an eye over an
under-nineteen net session in Lahore. He took ten wickets in his
second Test, and after starting at number eleven he was soon
working his way up the batting order. For Pakistan against
Zimbabwe at Sheikhupura in 1996, batting at number eight, he
made 257 not out, an innings that contained twelve sixes and is
the highest score in Test cricket by anyone going in lower than
number five. His bat, one of the heaviest in the game, is as much
a cannon as a piece of sporting equipment.

ENGLAND, PAST AND PRESENT
1770–1900

(After reading Nyren's *Young Cricketer's Tutor*)

BUT for an hour to watch them play,
  Those heroes dead and gone,
And pit our batsmen of to-day
  With those of Hambledon!
Our *Graces, Nyrens, Studds,* and *Wards,*
  In weeks of sunny weather,
Somewhere upon Elysian swards,
  To see them matched together!

Could we but see how *SMALL* withstands
  The three-foot break of *Steel,*
If *Silver Billy's* 'wondrous hands'
  Survive with *Briggs* or *Peel!*
If *Mann,* with all his pluck of yore,
  Can keep the leather rolling,
And, at a crisis, notch a score,
  When *Woods* and *Hearne* are bowling!

No doubt the *Doctor* would bewitch
  His quaint top-hatted foes,
Though, on a deftly chosen pitch,
  Old *Harris* bowled his slows;
And *Aylward,* if the asphodel
  Had made the wicket bumpy,
Would force the game with *Attewell,*
  And *Stoddart* collar '*Lumpy*'

When Time of all our flannelled hosts
  Leaves only the renown,
Our cracks, perhaps, may join the ghosts
  That roam on Windmill Down,
Where shadowy crowds will watch the strife,
  And cheer the deeds of wonder
Achieved by giants whom in life
  A century kept asunder.

ALFRED COCHRANE

61

John **Small**

*'. . . defended with a straighter bat than
anyone had before him . . .'*

Of the members of cricket's first great side, the Hambledon club, none was more prominent or is recalled with more affection than John Small, born in Petersfield in 1737. He sold his wicket just as dearly as any Bailey, Bannerman or Boycott.

First a shoemaker, then a gamekeeper, a fine skater and a good musician, he spent his spare time making bats and balls. Hung above his house was a painted sign, stating:

> Here lives John Small,
> Makes Bat and ball,
> Pitch a wicket,
> Play at cricket,
> With any man in England.

And because he defended with a straighter bat than anyone had before him, his became the most prized wicket in the land. Once, playing for Hambledon against All-England, he kept up his wicket for all three days of the match, and when, on another occasion, he was bowled by 'Lumpy' Stevens, it was said to be the first time for several years that anyone had done it. Indeed, the change whereby cricket became a three-stump game had not a little to do with Small's immovability when there were only two.

The change followed a match played for high stakes on the Artillery Ground at Finsbury (the first ground in London where big cricket was played) between five men of Hambledon and five of Kent. Each side was allowed a 'given man' and Kent's was the same 'Lumpy' Stevens, who several times beat Small all ends up only to see the ball go between the two stumps, set six to eight inches apart.

62

Allan Gibson **Steel**

*'. . . the personification of the
nineteenth-century amateur.'*

In his I Zingari cap and ample moustache, his shirt buttoned at
the neck and the cuffs, A.G. Steel was the personification of the
nineteenth-century amateur. Even when he was still a boy at
Marlborough he was said to be good enough to be in the England
side, and in 1878, his first year at Cambridge, he headed the
national bowling averages with 164 wickets at 9.43 apiece.

The following year, Steel and the Oxonian, A.H. Evans,
bowled unchanged through both innings for the Gentlemen
against the Players at the Oval. The Players made 73 and 48 on
what Wisden described as 'a treacherous pitch'. Had he not been
so keen to head north for the grouse moors come the Twelfth
of August, and then committed himself to a legal career (he was
the Recorder of Oldham when he died at the age of fifty-five),
Steel would almost certainly have played more than the thirteen
Test matches that he did.

He bowled quickish, accurate leg-breaks, mixed with the
occasional off-break and the odd very fast ball, and he was a good
enough attacking batsman to score 135 not out in a Test match
at Sydney and 148 in the Lord's Test of 1884, also against
Australia. Steel was the bowler during the Scarborough Festival
when C.I. Thornton hit the ball into that fair town's Trafalgar
Square, a hugely tall and quite exceptionally long carry. When
Thornton was boasting of it some years later to a lady whose
attention had wandered, she enquired in astonishment: 'From
Lord's, Mr Thornton, or the Oval?'

63

Geoffrey **Boycott**

*'. . . attracted either fanatical support
or uncompromising opposition.'*

Geoffrey Boycott rather enjoyed being the most contentious sporting figure of his day. To some he was 'Sir Geoffrey', to others more of a thundering bore. Brian Clough, then England's best-known football manager, was of the former persuasion, Denis Compton, ever the toreador, was of the latter. Of the 112 batsmen to have made more than 25,000 first-class runs, only Don Bradman (28,067 at 95.14) has a higher career average than Boycott (48,426 at 56.83); but Boycott's Test average of 47.72 is more modest.

In a sense, he spent much of his career living down the sparkling century he made at Lord's in the Gillette Cup final of 1965, when he was young and bespectacled. Only very seldom after that did he really let himself go. Instead, he accumulated runs with an intensity of purpose, a profusion and a wariness that invited charges, almost inevitably, of self-interest. Even in his native Yorkshire he attracted either fanatical support or uncompromising opposition, and not all his colleagues appreciated being summoned to some strange places, such as the one illustrated here, to satisfy his obsession with practice.

But almost to a man the country regretted it when, in the disappointment of being passed over for the England captaincy, he made himself unavailable for Test matches from 1974 until 1977. It was another sign of the intransigence that made him the player he was – not a great one in the glorious sense but a marvel all the same. Today, as a commentator on radio and television, he has cast off all his inhibitions.

64

Thomas Godfrey **Evans**

'. . . a wonderful way of communicating optimism and vitality.'

For anyone fond of cricket but feeling down in the dumps, there was no better tonic during the 1950s than to go and see Godfrey Evans keeping wicket for Kent or England. He had a wonderful way of communicating optimism and vitality, on top of which he was a brilliant practitioner.

The one and only "GODDERS"

However unpromising the outlook, Evans was never downhearted. After England had lost the First Test at Brisbane in 1954–55 by a horrendous margin, a match which he himself had missed through illness, he was almost more buoyant than his troubled captain, Len Hutton, could take. 'Don't you worry,' he used to say, 'we'll be there at the finish.' And in the next three Tests on that tour, that is just where he was: he put an end to Australia's resistance with diving leg-side catches off Frank Tyson in the Second and Third Tests and hit the winning run in the Fourth.

Evans's wicket-keeping on the previous MCC tour of Australia, standing up to Alec Bedser and coping with the waspish but wayward leg-breaks and googlies of Doug Wright, touched perfection. He was very sturdy and very quick – so quick with his leg-side stumpings that spectators were sometimes left wondering what had happened when they saw the batsman leaving the wicket. He made bad returns look respectable and gave the batsman never a moment's respite, not by today's endless chatter but simply by being so good. Against India at Lord's in 1952 he scored 104, 98 of them before lunch on the third day, the innings of a hard and adventurous hitter.

65

Michael Anthony **Holding**

*'Had he not taken to cricket, he might well have
joined the company of great Jamaican athletes.'*

Of the coterie of West Indian fast bowlers, none has been more
effortlessly effective than Michael Holding. He was known in the
game as 'whispering death' on account of his silent, perfectly
balanced, distinctly feline run-up. Had he not taken to cricket,
he might well have joined the company of great Jamaican athletes.

There was never a much finer exhibition of sustained fast
bowling than Holding's against England at the Oval in 1976. No
small part of its beauty was its fullness of length. A month earlier,
in the Test match at Old Trafford, he had figured no less prominently in a shameful hour of ceaseless, unchecked intimidation.

But in capturing fourteen wickets for 149 runs at the Oval,
he was more concerned with making the ball swing than the
batsman duck: of the seven batsmen whose stumps he hit, four
were yorked. When you think that there were times in the 1980s
when Andy Roberts, Joel Garner and Malcolm Marshall were all
in the same side as Holding, it is no wonder that West Indies so
pulverized their opponents. Not since Mill Reef won the Derby
has anything covered the ground more smoothly than Michael
Holding, whether he was playing for West Indies, Jamaica,
Derbyshire, Lancashire, Tasmania or Canterbury.

66

Learie Nicholas **Constantine**

'. . . one of the game's greatest celebrities.'

Learie Constantine, known affectionately in the cricket world as 'Connie', was a pioneer among West Indian cricketers. He was not a consistently great batsman, nor a consistently great bowler, but he was breathtaking in the field and undoubtedly one of the game's greatest celebrities.

Coming to England for the first time in 1923, when he was twenty, he became a regular visitor, either with official West Indies sides, or to play for Nelson in the Lancashire League, or as a politician, or to be called to the Bar, or as the High Commissioner for Trinidad and Tobago, or first to be knighted and eventually ennobled. For their first Test victory over England, at Georgetown in 1929–30, West Indies were indebted to Constantine and George Headley, another of their cricketing legends. Headley scored a century in each innings and Constantine took nine wickets in the match. At times he was very fast; but because he was so consistently inventive, his bowling, like his batting, was spectacularly unpredictable.

In 1928 he was one of only three touring cricketers in this century to have completed the double of 1,000 runs and 100 wickets in an English season (Warwick Armstrong for the Australians in 1905 and Vinoo Mankad for the Indians in 1946 are the others), and he signed off at the Oval in 1939, in his last Test match, with five for seventy-nine in England's first innings, followed by a whirlwind 79 in a little over an hour. He was a wonderful entertainer, as talented as any of the great West Indians to have since danced in his unprompted footsteps.

67

Clive Hubert **Lloyd**

*'. . . great height and strength, and
a custom-built bat . . .'*

When Clive Lloyd cut loose with the bat it was an experience which the fielding captain and his bowlers were never likely to forget. It must have been much the same when another very tall left-hander with an equally unstinting swing of the bat, Frank Woolley, was making his 150s in a couple of hours for Kent, half a century earlier.

Lloyd flayed the bowling, using his great height and strength and a heavy, custom-built bat to scatter the field. In large glasses and with more of a lope than a walk, he hardly looked the part; yet he became a figure of huge influence in the game. Having established himself by making 127 in his first Test match against Australia and 118 in his first against England, and by fielding as dominantly and dynamically in the covers as anyone ever can have, he went on to lead West Indies seventy-four times and to create a formula which made them, for a full decade, well-nigh impregnable.

This consisted of their fielding four very good, very fast bowlers, who were in plentiful supply in the Caribbean at the time, and of the often indiscriminate use of short-pitched bowling. Lloyd conducted operations from slip, made runs down the order when they were needed and became a paterfamilias to his adoring players. Without the fast bowlers to demolish the opposition, he found life much more difficult as Lancashire's captain from 1981 to 1983 and after that as manager of the West Indian Test side.

A New Zealander by birth, Clarrie Grimmett moved to Australia when he was twenty-two in search of cricketing opportunities, and even then he needed all his perseverance to find them. When, eventually, he did so, the results were spectacular.

He was a very small, rather beaky, prematurely wizened, totally dedicated wrist-spinner, who bowled with a jerky round-arm action, tantalizing accuracy and a drifting flight. He had to wait until he was thirty-three before being awarded an Australian cap, but in his first Test match, against England at Sydney in 1924–25, he took eleven for eighty-two, and he went on to become the first bowler ever to take 200 Test wickets. His final tally of 216 stood as an Australian record until Ray Lindwall broke it twenty-three years later, having played twenty more Test matches than 'Grum'.

With Bill O'Reilly, Grimmett formed the most effective spin-bowling partnership of all time: in the fifteen Tests they played together – eight against England and seven against South Africa – they shared 169 wickets, Grimmett taking 88 of them and O'Reilly 81. They became, into the bargain, the closest of friends, a picture of dignity and impudence.

Grimmett was still breaking records in his fiftieth year, and still working to refine and develop the art of leg-spin bowling to the advantage of the Doolands and the Benauds and the Warnes and all the others who were to follow him in the practice of it. The 'flipper' – the ball which comes out from under the wrist and hurries on to the batsman along the angle of its flight – was Grimmett's invention.

68

Clarence Victor **Grimmett**

'. . . a jerky round-arm action and a drifting flight.'

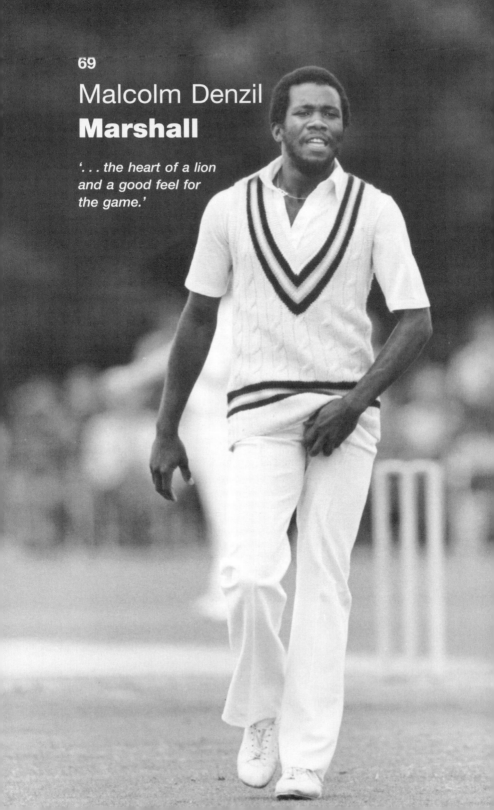

69

Malcolm Denzil
Marshall

*'... the heart of a lion
and a good feel for
the game.'*

Take any twelve West Indian fast bowlers and the odd man out, physically anyway, is almost sure to be Malcolm Marshall. The only other one of distinction who was anything like as small was another Barbadian, 'Manny' Martindale, way back in the 1930s.

Marshall had great natural resources. He had lissomness and rhythm, not so much in his run-up, which developed into something of a sprint, but in his delivery. He was a tireless competitor, not without his moods but with the heart of a lion and a good feel for the game. Although he bowled a horrid bouncer, which rather skidded through because of his lack of height, he was at his best when pitching the ball up and making it swing.

The only bowlers of anything like comparable speed to have taken as many as Marshall's 1,637 first-class wickets are Fred Trueman and Brian Statham, and perhaps Tom Richardson, who was obviously capable of great pace. Marshall's wickets were taken for West Indies, Barbados, Hampshire and Natal, the last of which he captained at the end of his playing career. As coach to the West Indies side since his retirement, and having become accustomed to their virtual invincibility in his playing days, he must have despaired at their recent lapses.

70

James Charles **Laker**

*'It made him, overnight, one of
the legends of the game.'*

If cricket is played for another thousand years Jim Laker's nineteen wickets for ninety runs for England against Australia at Old Trafford in 1956 will surely remain the most remarkable Test bowling analysis ever recorded. It made him, overnight, one of the legends of the game.

By playing in the days when pitches in England were left uncovered, he had the incomparable advantage of bowling his off-breaks on turf drying out after rain, sometimes under the pyrogenic influence of a hot sun. It didn't happen often, but when it did it meant that the initiative was wholly with the bowler, and in such circumstances, as on that famous occasion at Old Trafford, Laker was without peer. Six years earlier, at Bradford, within five miles of where he was born, he had ruined a Test Trial by returning figures, for England against The Rest, of 14 overs – 12 maidens – 2 runs – 8 wickets – on the first morning of the match.

But even on a shirt-front of a pitch, both in England and overseas, he was very seldom collared. He would jog into bowl, his weight on his heels; he knew the value of the pivot, and with a condescending air he probed a batsman's weakness. One associates him not so much with flight, or even subtlety, as with spin and composure and the exercise of control.

71

Waqar **Younis**

*'. . . he introduced a new and
at times deadly variant . . .'*

Born in the Punjab but brought up in Sharjah, Waqar Younis became the talk of the cricket world in the course of a year. At the age of eighteen he had the good fortune to be seen on television, bowling in a local knock-out game, by Imran Khan, who, as Pakistan's captain, made it his business to find out more about him.

Very soon Waqar was on a learning tour of Australia with the full Pakistan side, and it was on Imran's recommendation that Surrey then took him on. 'In a year when batsmen reigned supreme, Surrey spent much of the summer of 1990 admiring their rare and unexpected gift from the Orient,' said *Wisden* at the end of Waqar's first season with them. With reverse swing (swing, that is, against the shinier side of the ball), bowled at high speed and to a full length, he introduced a new and at times deadly variant into the game. His first 33 Tests brought him 190 wickets at a striking rate of a wicket every 40 balls, one that had been unapproached since the very different days of S.F. Barnes. So pronounced and unconventional was Waqar's swing that his method became, for a while, a source of wonder, not to say suspicion.

But almost inevitably the exigencies of fast bowling were to take their toll. A complaining back forced him to miss whole tours, and his rhythm duly suffered. He was then temporarily deprived, by his country's cricketing machinations, of his longstanding and most famous bowling partner, Wasim Akram. Waqar has been, for all that, one of the game's most pulverizing forces, with an inswinging yorker that was as likely to shatter a batsman's instep as to send a stump flying.

72

David Ivon **Gower**

'. . . one of only five England captains in the last sixty-five years to have regained The Ashes.'

David Gower was the most graceful batsman of his generation. He pulled his first ball in Test cricket nonchalantly for four and still looked full of delightful runs when the England selectors lost faith in him fourteen years later. They were trying a more ascetic line, and decided that on balance Gower's contribution would not be for the good.

It was a sad and inexpedient end, though to some extent he brought it upon himself by his outwardly casual ways. His style at the crease was such that what was interpreted as indifference was often more of a mannerism. There was usually a certain amount of playing and missing outside the off stump, but that is an occupational hazard of the left-handed batsman, and even during his most restrained innings, such as his unbeaten 154 in seven and three-quarter hours to save a Test match in Jamaica, one's heart tended to be in one's mouth.

Gower's timing was pure genius. His philosophy was the same as W.G.'s: 'Let's get at them before they get at us.' It allowed him to make eighteen Test hundreds, and he stands second only to Graham Gooch in the number of runs made for England in Test cricket. In the natural course of things the captaincy came his way, and between December 1984 and September 1985 he led England to victory in India and became one of only five England captains in the last sixty-five years to have regained the Ashes. But that, too, ended unhappily and unhelpfully. There developed, thereafter, an incompatibility between the functionalism of Gooch, Gower's successor as captain, and the allure of Gower that did nothing whatever for England's cause.

Charles Thomas Biass
Turner

*'. . . became known on both sides of
the world as "the Terror".'*

Considering how amazingly successful a bowler he was, it is
surprising how little impact the name of C.T.B. Turner makes
today. No other Australian has taken a hundred wickets in so
few Test matches (seventeen, all against strong England batting
sides) or had such a tour of England as Turner did in 1888. In
that season alone – an admittedly wet one – he took 283 first-
class wickets at 11.68 apiece, mostly with balls that cut back from
the off. Against an England X1 at the Hastings Festival he took
seventeen wickets for fifty runs, of which fourteen were bowled,
two were leg-before and one was stumped; and in the three Tests
he took twenty-one wickets at 12.42 a time.

Still the only man ever to have taken a hundred wickets in
an Australian season, Turner became known on both sides of the
world as 'the Terror', just as Spofforth was 'the Demon'. Yet he
is not a part of the lore of the game in the same way as Spofforth.

Unorthodox actions quite often produce surprisingly effective results, and Turner's delivery was very open-chested, his arm
very low. This makes it the more surprising that he should have
gained sufficient pace off the ground to draw particular comment
from both W.G. and F.S. Jackson. Through the air Turner's pace
was of no real consequence, other than in the way that he varied
it. But he did bowl on uncovered pitches, which greatly bene-
fited him, and in the days when pad play, as a defensive measure,
was seldom practiced.

Archibald Campbell
Maclaren

'He played in the grand manner . . .'

There is not a name more redolent of cricket's Golden Age than A.C. Maclaren's. Adapting Shakespeare, Neville Cardus called him 'the noblest Roman of them all'.

Although he led England twenty-two times and took the side to Australia in 1901–02, and was a thorough student of the game, Archie Maclaren was not one of the great captains. He may have been too autocratic for that, and not sufficiently inclined to seek advice. But he was a truly commanding and enduringly influential figure. Even in his fiftieth year, when he said he could take a side into the field, comprising eleven amateurs, to beat Warwick Armstrong's all-conquering Australians in 1921, he was given the chance to do so and duly pulled off a famous victory.

Less than a month after captaining Harrow against Eton at Lord's in 1890, he scored 108 for Lancashire against Sussex at Hove; he made his first tour to Australia when he was twenty-two, and scored 424 for Lancashire against Somerset at Taunton when he was twenty-three, an innings that contained sixty-four fours and one six. For twenty-seven years this was the record first-class score.

Right up to the Second World War there were Australians who said Maclaren was the finest English batsman ever to visit them, Hammond and Hobbs notwithstanding. He played in the grand manner, standing tall, lifting the bat very high, following through with a flourish and always looking to attack. After watching Maclaren and C.B. Fry add 309 in just under three hours for the Gentlemen against the Players in 1903, Cardus wrote that he had never seen batting of 'such opulence and prerogative'.

Alfred **Shaw**

'. . . line, length and little changes of pace.'

Perhaps Alfred Shaw's greatest claim to fame is the fact that he clean bowled W.G. twenty times in first-class cricket, six times more than the next man, who was Tom Richardson. He did so at what today might be considered a very gentle, not to say vulnerable, medium-pace.

Shaw played from 1864 until 1897, his virtues being the simple but everlasting ones of line, length and little changes of pace. Until the turn of the century and beyond, most village sides in England would have fielded someone of the same portly build as Shaw and bowling in much the same way. So long as he kept pitching the ball on the proverbial sixpence, it seemed not to matter how much weight he put on or how old he was.

For most of his career, an over consisted of four balls, and it was very rare that the runs he conceded outnumbered the overs he bowled. He had seventeen years on the MCC groundstaff and played until he was fifty-five, bowling, all told, 24,700 overs from which 16,922 runs were scored, and taking 2,027 wickets at an average of 12.12. In the last of the three Gentlemen and Players matches of 1877, played at Prince's, Shaw's figures at the end of the first day were three wickets (including W.G.'s) for twelve runs from forty-eight overs.

With Arthur Shrewsbury and James Lillywhite, Shaw took three strong all-professional sides to Australia, in the first of which, at Melbourne on 15 March 1877, he bowled the first ball in what was later to be recognized as the first Test Match of all – another of his indisputable claims to fame.

Gilbert Laird **Jessop**

'. . . scored his runs at a scarcely believable eighty an hour . . .'

Every generation brings to light its great and fearless hitters of a cricket ball. The 1980s, for example, could claim Ian Botham, Kapil Dev and Vivian Richards. Yet not even one of these could have outshone Gilbert Jessop of Cheltenham Grammar School, Cambridge University, Gloucestershire and England, who played from 1894 until 1914.

If he is best known for the 104 which he scored in seventy-five minutes on a none-too-easy pitch to win the Oval Test match against Australia in 1902, there were countless other innings in which Jessop flayed famous bowlers. Of his fifty-three first-class hundreds, no fewer than twelve were made in under an hour. Over his whole career he is said to have scored his runs at a scarcely believable eighty an hour, even though, until 1910, the ball had to be hit clean out of the ground to be counted as a six. Walter Brearley once got so cross with him that he bowled six balls in a row at or over his head, something that would never be countenanced today. Yet, although the England selectors were inclined to think so, Jessop was no mere slogger.

The son of a country doctor, he had very strong hands and long arms, and he adopted a crouching stance, with one hand near the top of the bat handle and the other right at the bottom. Upon having him in his Gloucestershire side for the first time, W.G. declared: 'Well, we've found something this time.' And Jessop was much more than a remarkable batsman. He was chosen for his first Test match, against Australia at Lord's in 1899, chiefly as an opening bowler, besides which he was the finest cover point of his day. And with it all, he was modesty itself.

Gilbert L Jessop.

77

John Brian **Statham**

'. . . amazingly easy-going.'

Brian Statham was an extraordinarily accurate, extensively double-jointed and amazingly easy-going fast bowler. There can never have been one who was either more popular or sent down fewer loose balls.

He was only twenty and a mere slip of a lad, who had bowled fewer than 300 overs in first-class cricket, when he was flown out to Australia in January 1951 to reinforce F.R. Brown's injury-ridden MCC side. His selection was based on an opening spell for Lancashire in the 1950 Roses match at Old Trafford which Wisden said 'bordered on the sensational'. On going back to Australia four years later, Statham formed a fast-bowling partnership with Frank Tyson of unforeseen and memorable impact. Although Tyson took twenty-eight wickets in the Tests of 1954–55 to Statham's eighteen, Statham's contribution was every bit as important. Because of his great speed Tyson was invariably given the down-wind end, but Statham's stamina and good nature and commitment could put up with that.

England were never better served for fast bowling than in the 1950s, and Statham was always there, hitting the right spot and moving the ball this way and that simply by doing what came naturally. He was also a lovely fielder out in the country, with a fast and effortless return. His occasional, always genial, appearances on the tennis court revealed the same balance and rhythm.

78

Vintcent Adriaan Pieter
van der Bijl

*'. . . the best fast or fastish bowler
never to play Test cricket.'*

Only South Africa's exclusion from Test cricket
between 1970 and 1992 prevented Vintcent van
der Bijl from becoming the Curtly Ambrose of his
day, and just as widely feared and highly rated.
Ambrose is 6ft 7ins tall; van der Bijl was half an
inch taller and every bit as accurate. The South
African's average length was significantly fuller
than the West Indian's, but his bounce was just as
steep.

Not even any of the great South African
googly bowlers, bowling on matting pitches in the
early years of this century, had figures to compare
with van der Bijl's. All the major bowling records
in domestic first-class cricket in South Africa
belong to him, and when he decided to measure
himself in a more professional school by having
one season with Middlesex in the county championship, he reinforced, indeed enhanced, his
reputation.

Mike Brearley, his Middlesex captain, described van der Bijl's contribution, both as cricketer and enthusiast, as 'the biggest single factor'
behind their winning the 1980 championship. Few
were left in any doubt after that that they had seen
the best fast or fastish bowler never to play Test
cricket. Only devotees of J. Barton King, the great
Philadelphian, might not agree.

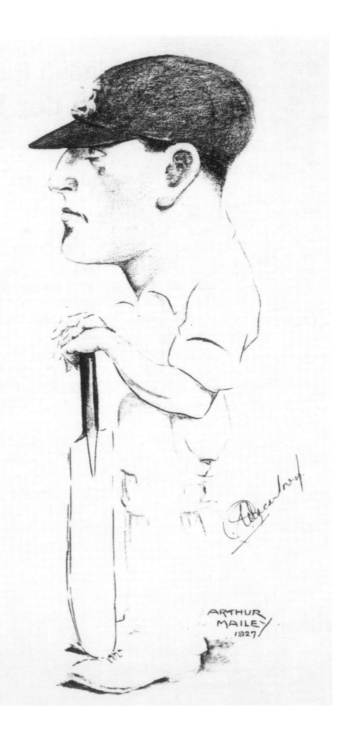

ARTHUR
MAILEY
1927

79

Charles George **Macartney**

'. . . known as the "Governor General"
or, by some, as "His Eminence".'

In nearly 300 Tests between England and Australia only three batsmen have launched a match with a century before lunch on the first day, and they were all Australians. Victor Trumper did it at Old Trafford in 1902, C.G. Macartney at Headingley in 1926 and Don Bradman at Headingley in 1930.

Whereas Trumper had gone in first, Bradman and Macartney both went in at the fall of the first wicket. Arthur Carr had put Australia in when Macartney cut loose, a much less common practice then than it is now, and Warren Bardsley was caught at slip off the first ball of the match, bowled by Maurice Tate. Off the fifth ball of the same over Macartney was dropped where Bardsley had been caught, also by Carr, a chance that was to become a part of cricket lore.

By this time in his career – he was past his fortieth birthday – Charlie Macartney allowed nothing to stand in the way of his attacking inclinations. In his early Test matches he had been more of a slow left-arm bowler and an occasionally dour batsman. But after the Great War his batting was so transformed that he became known as the 'Governor General' or, by some, as 'His Eminence'. The word which by then characterized his batting was audaciousness. He hated playing a maiden over, often producing strokes that were in no textbook in order to prevent it. Squarely built and very strong, he was described once as an 'individual genius, not in any way to be copied' – an earlier version, perhaps, of the great West Indian, Vivian Richards.

80

Robert Baddeley **Simpson**

'. . . as hard as a pebble . . .'

For close on forty years, ending in 1996, Australia's cricketing fortunes were in and out of the hands of Bobby Simpson. Of Scottish extraction (his father played professional football for Stenhousemuir) he inclined towards an always canny, sometimes dour game, first as a highly organized batsman and brilliant slip fielder who also bowled useful leg-breaks, then as Australia's captain and finally as their coach.

For such an instinctive, single-minded and prolific batsman, he was a surprisingly long time making the first of his ten Test hundreds. It took him fifty-two innings, but when it arrived, against England at Old Trafford in 1964, it was no ordinary affair, lasting, as it did, for 12 hours 42 minutes, the longest innings ever played for Australia, and ending only when he had made 311, the eleventh highest individual score in Test cricket.

Having retired in 1968, Simpson was persuaded to come back in 1977 when Australian cricket was thrown into confusion by the defection of a majority of their best players to Kerry Packer's extravaganza. At the ripe old age of forty-two, therefore, Simpson found himself leading a side of striplings in the Caribbean against the full might of a hostile, Packer-affiliated West Indian attack. Never having shirked confrontation, and being as hard as a pebble, he was prepared to die with his boots on, as he might well have had to do from a blow by a rising cricket ball. When, eventually, he put his pads away, he teamed up with one of his protégés, Allan Border, to put Australian cricket together again.

Getting on for seven feet tall and delivering the ball with pinpoint accuracy and good speed from a height of around ten feet, Curtly Ambrose has been one of the most consistently menacing bowlers not only of the last dozen years but of all time. Upon his retirement, batsmen the world over will sleep more easily.

As a sky-scraping teenager he thought of setting course for the United States and chancing his arm as a basketball player. This is something that more and more would-be West Indian fast bowlers are doing, much to the detriment of cricket in the Caribbean. But Andy Roberts, Ambrose's fellow Antiguan and himself a greatly feared fast bowler, took him in hand, and Ambrose stayed put. For most of the 1990s West Indies would have been lost without him.

A familiar sound in Swetes, the village in Antigua from which Ambrose hails, is that of a bell being rung by his mother, at all hours of the day or the night (according to the country from which the radio commentary is coming), to announce the fall of another wicket to her stratospheric son. A stern and unrelenting opponent, he has rapped many a finger and many a rib with his often almost vertical bounce; but his yorker is just as destructive, and if he bowls

a long hop or a full toss he can scarcely believe it. When he does so, his fielders know to give him a wide berth.

Curtly Elconn Lynwall
Ambrose

'A stern and unrelenting opponent . . .'

Fazal **Mahmood**

*'. . . the last great bowler on the mat,
whether of coir or jute . . .'*

The last Test match to be played on a matting
pitch was at Karachi in December 1950 (watched,
as it happens, by Dwight D. Eisenhower, the then
President of the United States), and the last great
bowler on the mat, whether of coir or jute, was
Fazal Mahmood. It was a surface which gave
purchase to the ball. The slacker the mat the greater
the purchase, and the greater the purchase the
deadlier Fazal became.

When Australia played Pakistan for the first
time, at Karachi in 1956 on their way home from
England, they were bowled out for 80 and 187,
Fazal taking thirteen wickets for 114 runs. Matting
laid on concrete produced bounce; laid on turf, as
in Karachi, it did not, and it was here that Fazal's
ability to cut the ball either way at medium pace
and to bowl with unerring accuracy made him
uniquely effective.

But he was also a fine bowler on turf pitches.
At the Oval in 1954, for example, his twelve for
ninety-nine enabled Pakistan, making their first
tour of England, to achieve one of the least
expected victories in Test history, and even in the
West Indies he was never collared. Of the 186 overs
he bowled in successive Test matches in Trinidad
and Jamaica against, among others, Rohan Kanhai,
Gary Sobers, Clyde Walcott and Everton Weekes in
1957–58, sixty-five were maidens. After retiring
from cricket Fazal continued to keep order – as a
police superintendent.

83

William Harold **Ponsford**

'. . . extraordinary powers of concentration.'

As a maker of monumental individual scores, Bill Ponsford was pre-eminent until the young Don Bradman came along, and he is still the only batsman to have made two quadruple hundreds – 437 for Victoria against Queensland and 429 for Victoria against Tasmania. In his last two Test matches for Australia – against England at Headingley and the Oval in 1934 – he added 388 and 451 with Bradman, a series in which he averaged 94.83 to Bradman's 94.73. They were described at the time as being 'the thunder of Melbourne and the lightning of Sydney'.

In December 1927, Ponsford scored 1,146 runs in five Sheffield Shield innings for Victoria at an average of 229.20. For a time, therefore, he bore comparison with the most successful batsman in all history, not in style, his own being altogether more prosaic than the Don's, but in sheer weight of runs. Much about Ponsford – his bat, his pads, his hind-quarters, his defensive strokes – seemed abnormally broad, just as privately he was abnormally taciturn.

He was hit on the body by the fast bowlers more than he should have been, perhaps, and he was not renowned as a bad-wicket player; but he had extraordinary powers of concentration. When he played the ball on to his stumps after making 352 for Victoria against New South Wales at Melbourne in 1926, 'Ponny' remarked to the wicket-keeper, before trudging off to the pavilion, 'How unlucky can you get.'

84

Hanif **Mohammad**

'. . . a tiny, tenacious, inscrutable,
inspirational figure.'

For thirty-five years Hanif Mohammad held two of the most spectacular of all individual batting records. His 499 for Karachi against Bahawalpur at Karachi in January 1960 was the highest score ever made (he was run out, looking to keep the bowling!) and his 337 in sixteen hours and ten minutes for Pakistan against West Indies at Bridgetown in January 1958 was the longest innings ever played. The second of these records survives by nearly three hours; the first stands today to Brian Lara by reason of his 501 not out for Warwickshire against Durham at Edgbaston in 1994.

Of Pakistan's first fifty-seven Test matches Hanif played in fifty-five. Time and again he stood on the burning deck – a tiny, tenacious, inscrutable, inspirational figure. His 337, Test cricket's fifth highest score, was made after Pakistan had followed on 473 runs behind West Indies, and it forced a highly improbable draw. Against England at Lord's in 1967 he made 187 not out in Pakistan's first innings after they had been 99 for six, and that match, too, was drawn.

More than anyone, Hanif, Fazal Mahmood and Hafeez Kardar put Pakistani cricket on the map; but only Hanif has ever had three brothers (Mushtaq, Sadiq and Wazir) and a son (Shoaib) who were also Test players. As a boy, Hanif was taught the art of survival against the turning ball when his coach created the necessary conditions by dousing the good length of a practice pitch.

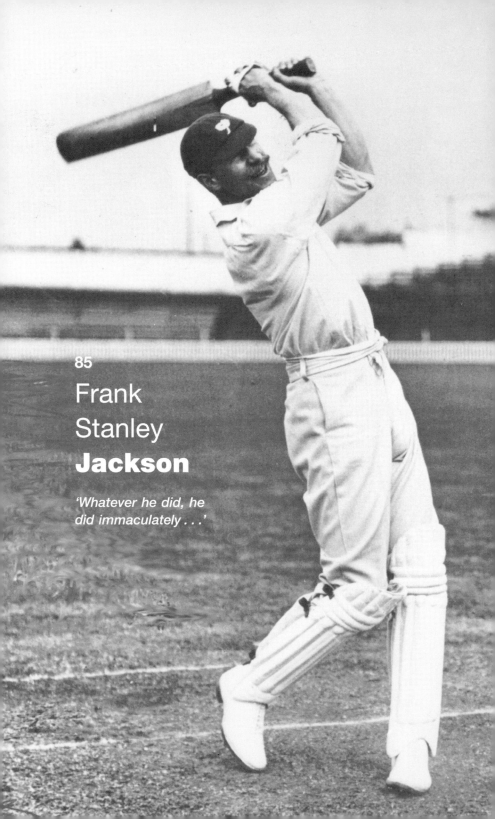

85
Frank
Stanley
Jackson

'Whatever he did, he did immaculately . . .'

A very fine batsman, a successful captain of England, a Member of Parliament for eleven years, commander of his battalion in the Great War, and an imperturbable Governor of Bengal (during his time in Calcutta he survived, with sang froid, an attempt on his life), Sir Stanley Jackson was some all-rounder. It was after leading England to victory over Australia in 1905 that he went into politics.

He was still up at Cambridge when he made 91 at Lord's in the first of his twenty Test matches and 103 at the Oval in the second. He only ever played for England at home and then only against Australia, and the 1905 series, the one in which he was captain, was in every way his best. He averaged 70 with the bat and took thirteen wickets at fifteen apiece. At a time when English batsman-ship led the world, Jackson, when available, was an auto-matic choice.

Whatever he did, he did immaculately: his strokes, his moustache, his manner, his style, his appearance were all beautifully groomed, and he had the best of tempera-ments. C.B. Fry said he delighted in Jackson's captaincy, and in the fact that he batted as well on mud as on marble. In the House of Commons, when Jackson was due to make his maiden speech, the Speaker passed him a note, saying: 'I've dropped you in the batting order, it's a sticky wicket at the moment.' Later, when the situation eased, he sent him another, saying: 'Get your pads on, you're in next.'

86

Robert George Dylan **Willis**

'. . . went on to surpass all expectations.'

Two factors contributed most to Bob Willis's splendid collection of 325 Test wickets, 128 of them against Australia – his height and an immense determination. One would have been no good without the other.

He was that modern rarity – a frequently successful, genuinely fast English bowler. In the last thirty-five years the only other has been John Snow. Almost inevitably Willis's long back – he was 6ft 6ins tall – gave him trouble; but he got the better of it, sparing himself nothing in the process, and went on to surpass all expectations.

The famous Headingley Test match of 1981 may be thought of as having belonged to Ian Botham; but without Willis's eight for forty-three on the last day, with Australia needing only 130 to win, England's great victory could never have happened.

At the time, Willis's place in the England side was far from secure. He had bowled very little in 1980, owing to injury, and had been obliged to opt out of the tour to West Indies in the winter of 1980–81. Then came Headingley, and within a year his installation as England's captain. He led them eighteen times, five of those in Australia, without ever seeming at ease in the job. Fast bowling and captaincy have seldom gone comfortably together.

THE LION-TAMER.

87

Warwick Windridge
Armstrong

'. . . known to all and sundry as the "Big Ship".'

The Australian Board of Control must have heaved a collective sigh of relief when Warwick Armstrong retired, for he was never afraid to call them to account; but he had a very fine all-round record as a powerful batsman and a leg-break bowler, and he was unbeaten as a Test captain, albeit at a time when England were rebuilding after the Great War.

When he took the field in his first Test match, in 1901–02, Armstrong weighed less than eleven stone; when he left it in his fiftieth and last Test he was almost exactly twice as heavy and was known to all and sundry as the 'Big Ship'. No ball driven by him, nor deck chair he sat in, was reckoned ever to be quite the same again. Even now, one of the favourite exhibits at the Melbourne Cricket Ground is the last of his cricket shirts: it could be hired out as a marquee.

In England in 1905 Armstrong scored 1,902 runs and took 122 wickets, as productive a double as was ever achieved by any touring cricketer. In three of the Test matches that year he incurred some disfavour by bowling long spells of negative leg-breaks pitched outside the leg stump to a strong on-side field, as is being done with increasing frequency today. In 1912 he was one of six leading Australian players who refused to tour England through being denied the right to choose their own manager, and when the Oval Test match of 1921 was drawing to its uneventful close he began to read an evening paper that had been blown on to the field. 'I wanted to see who we were playing,' he said afterwards. He was, for all that, very kindhearted and unfailingly loyal to his players.

88

Derek Leslie **Underwood**

'. . . after rain he could be virtually unplayable.'

But for going off when in his prime, first to Australia to play for
Kerry Packer and then to South Africa on a 'rebel' tour, Derek
Underwood would almost certainly have become England's
leading Test wicket-taker and quite likely the leading one of all.

In the event he finished with 297 Test wickets as against
Ian Botham's 383 and Kapil Dev's unequalled 434. Underwood's
main assets were a rhythmical approach, great pride in his bowling and meticulous, almost metronomic, control. He was frugal
to a fault. For fear of overpitching, he seldom gave the ball much
air. Indeed, his prevailing pace was slow-medium. He was not,
therefore, a left-arm spinner in the classical sense. But there was
no one like him for closing down an end, and when the ball
turned, particularly after rain, he could be virtually unplayable.

He took a hundred first-class wickets for the first time in the
season of his eighteenth birthday, which was unprecedented for
anyone so young, and he was still only twenty-three when his
seven for fifty enabled England to gain a dramatic last-gasp
victory over Australia at the Oval in 1968 (pictured below,
sawdust and all). His 2,465 first-class wickets at 20.28 apiece are
850 more than anyone has taken who is playing today.

89

Sonny **Ramadhin**

'. . . a real touch of the conjuror about him.'

As a twenty-year-old, little known even in his native Trinidad, Sonny Ramadhin appeared from nowhere to confront England's batsmen with cricket's equivalent of the Rubic Cube. Their embarrassment was acute. It happened in 1950, the batsmen's problem being to distinguish Ramadhin's leg-break from his off-break, both of which he delivered from out of the front of the hand with his second finger down the seam.

As light and slight a bowler as ever played for West Indies, Ramadhin had a real touch of the conjuror about him. He bowled in a cap, with his sleeves rolled down, a quick arm and an enigmatic twirl of his fingers. So completely did he mesmerize England's batsmen when they first encountered him that his figures in only his second Test match were an extraordinary 115 overs – 70 maidens – 152 runs – 11 wickets. That was at Lord's of all places, and with Alf Valentine taking seven of the remaining nine wickets West Indies won their first-ever victory over England in England. Suddenly, at the top of the charts, there appeared a calypso:

> Cricket, lovely cricket,
> At Lord's where I saw it,
> Yardley* tried his best,
> Goddard* won the Test,
> With those little pals of mine,
> Ramadhin and Valentine.

In brighter climates than England's, batsmen could see which way Ramadhin was spinning the ball by watching it through the air, and eventually, at Edgbaston in 1957, in a partnership of 411, Peter May and Colin Cowdrey found their own solution; but Ramadhin had made, by then, an indelible mark on the game.

---

* Norman Yardley and John Goddard were the captains, respectively, of England and West Indies.

90

Lancelot Richard
Gibbs

'. . . a very short run and a very quick arm.'

Had he been born twenty years later, the chances are that Lance Gibbs would never have played cricket for West Indies. As it was, he bowled very nearly 1,000 more overs for them than anyone else has ever done, all off a very short run and with a very quick arm, and he took 309 Test wickets, a world record at the time and surpassed only by Shane Warne among slow bowlers.

Gibbs had the good fortune to come through in the late 1950s, when spin still counted for something in the Caribbean. The West Indian obsession with speed took hold soon after his last Test match in 1976, by when he was a greying but still lithe and wiry forty-one. By coincidence, the West Indian commitment to all-out, all-day pace was masterminded by Gibbs's fellow Guyanese and first cousin, Clive Lloyd.

Gibbs's strengths were spin, bounce, stamina and change of pace, and he used a long association with Warwickshire to overcome an aversion to bowling round the wicket, which had been holding him back. Having done with bowling for West Indies he went to live in the United States and bowled for them instead – against Canada in 1983. He also managed one or two West Indian Test sides, no doubt with itching fingers.

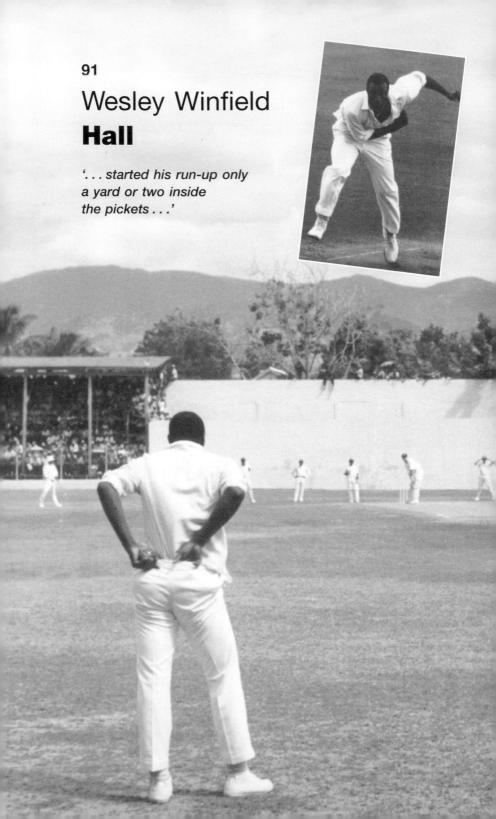

91

Wesley Winfield
Hall

*'. . . started his run-up only
a yard or two inside
the pickets . . .'*

Wesley Hall has been in his time a rampaging fast bowler with a matching sense of humour, Minister of Sport and then Tourism in his native Barbados and a God-fearing manager of the West Indies cricket team. When he played a season for Queensland in the Sheffield Shield they so took to him there that if he had stood for Mayor of Brisbane it was said that he would have romped home.

As a teenager he switched from keeping wicket to bowling fast when thrown the ball in the nets one day, and he went on to form, with Charlie Griffith, the first of the great West Indian fast bowling partnerships of the last forty years. They were the fore-runners of the giants of the 1980s, but whereas there were doubts about the legality of Griffith's action there were none regarding Hall's.

On the old Sabina Park ground in Jamaica, with its short straight bound-aries, Hall started his run-up only a yard or two inside the pickets, and his follow-through took him almost into the batsman's crease, arms and legs flying in all directions. He was a dramatic sight, with none of the smooth coordination of Holding and Marshall but every bit as much menace. For steadfastness and staying-power, his forty-six wickets in eight Test matches in India and Pakistan in 1958–59 at under eighteen runs apiece ranks with anything ever done there.

92

Mulvantrai Himmatlal
Mankad

'. . . took on England almost single-handed . . .'

For four days at Lord's in 1952 Vinoo Mankad took on England almost single-handed, and he was a reluctant hero. He had declined a place in the Indian side to England that year, opting instead for a more lucrative, less arduous summer playing for Haslingden in the Lancashire League, and it was from there that he rode to India's rescue after they had been heavily beaten in the First Test at Headingley.

At Lord's, in the Second Test, he scored 72 and 184 going in first, and bowled 97 overs of slow, languid, orthodox left arm spin, taking 5 for 231 in the process. England won comfortably in the end, but Mankad was unbowed. As a feat of all-round endurance it has seldom been equalled in Test cricket. Of the twenty-four and three-quarter hours for which the match lasted, Mankad spent twenty on the field of play.

At Melbourne in 1947–48 he made two Test hundreds against Australia, albeit in separate matches, and to this day his partnership of 413 with Pankaj Roy against New Zealand at Madras in 1955–56 is the world Test record for the first wicket. He had three sons who became first-class cricketers, one a Test cricketer, and still found time to play for a veritable directory of Indian states and English and Scottish clubs.

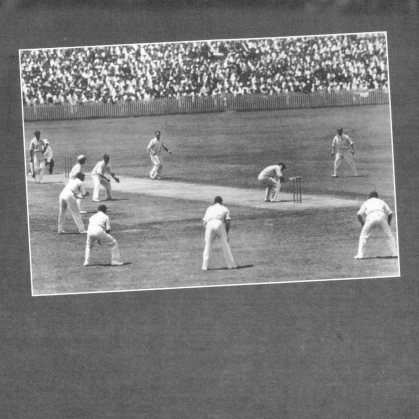

93

Harold **Larwood**

'In action he was a magnificent sight . . .'

Only 5ft 7⅝ins tall and never weighing more than ten and a half stone, Harold Larwood hardly had the build of a fast bowler; but he more than made up for that with the gathering momentum of his run-up, a perfect natural balance, long arms and a pair of shoulders strengthened by a couple of teenage years at the coalface in Nuncargate, the mining village in Nottinghamshire where he was born.

In action he was a magnificent sight; but what made him truly famous was bodyline, the method of attack devised by the England captain, Douglas Jardine, in Australia in 1932–33 to subdue the phenomenon that was Don Bradman. Larwood was its archetypal exponent, as much because of his accuracy as his speed. In that series alone he took 33 of his 78 Test wickets (including Bradman's four times), and, although 16 of them were clean bowled, the batsmen's ribs were at least as frequently Larwood's target as were the stumps.

Such was the acrimony this provoked that the tour, not to say Australia's allegiance to the Commonwealth, was threatened. Yet sixteen years later Larwood, his wife and four daughters emigrated to Australia, there to spend the last forty-five years of his life, eventually as 'one of them'. Having done his captain's bidding in Australia, Larwood never played for England again – partly through injury, partly through being badly advised and partly through cricket politics.

Jack Morrison **Gregory**

'. . . the Keith Miller of his day.'

For all too short a time Jack Gregory was the Keith Miller of his day. A member of a famous Australian cricketing dynasty, he was a dashing all-rounder – a fast right-arm bowler with a spectacular leap before delivering the ball, a flowing left-handed batsman and a flying slip-fielder.

Owing to the Great War, which began when he was just nineteen, and then to an increasingly troublesome knee, Gregory had only five years when he was at his best. The first of them was spent with the Australian Imperial Forces team in England in 1919. He had served in England and France in the war, and during a brief billeting at Lord's had met and impressed P.F. Warner (later Sir Pelham Warner). When peace returned and a side of Australian servicemen was being put together to play the English counties before returning home, Warner put Gregory's name forward.

This AIF tour, which also took in South Africa, was a personal triumph for Gregory. By the end of it he was an automatic choice for the first official post-war Australian side, although he had not yet played a first-class match at home. In only his second Test, against England at Melbourne in December 1920, he scored a century on the second day and took seven wickets for sixty-nine runs on the third, and he went on to form with the great Ted McDonald one of the most formidable of all fast bowling partnerships. In terms of time, as distinct from balls received, Gregory's 100 in seventy minutes against South Africa at Johannesburg in 1921–22 is still recognized as being the fastest in all Test cricket.

Stephen Rodger
Waugh

'. . . a temperament which responds to Test cricket.'

There is no more highly regarded cricketer playing the game today than Steve Waugh. His twin, Mark, has the flair to play the more captivating innings, but Steve has acquired the priceless knack of maximizing his ability.

This may have come from his having had to work harder at the game than his brother. He made the most of a season and a bit with Somerset when he was in his early twenties, getting into the way while he was there of making hundreds (eight in twenty-eight innings); but most important of all he has a temperament which responds to Test cricket. As England, South Africa and West Indies know to their cost, he is elevated by it.

Steve Waugh is the genuine article – a tough, tight-lipped Australian, who gives absolutely nothing away, least of all his own wicket. In his first 150 Test innings he was not out twenty-eight times. Believing that he was abnormally vulnerable to the bouncer, the West Indians have made a practice of bowling unmercifully short at him; but it was he who made the double-hundred in Kingston, Jamaica, in 1994–95 which finally unseated them after a decade and more of supremacy. Now, he has a hundred Test caps to his name, a Test batting average of very nearly 50 and the captaincy of Australia's one-day side.

96

Herbert Wilfred **Taylor**

'The England players marvelled at him.'

From all accounts, no bowling has ever been more consistently difficult to play than S.F. Barnes's for England in South Africa in 1913–14. In four Test matches he took forty-nine wickets at 10.93 runs each. According to Herbert Strudwick, the England wicket-keeper, he beat most of the South African batsmen two or three times an over. Yet Herbie Taylor, aged twenty-four, averaged 50.80 in the Test series, going in first. The England players marvelled at him.

The pitches were of matting on gravel, and from his considerable height Barnes made the ball both kick and turn. Taylor said that he was helped in reading Barnes's spin by having been brought up against the great South African googly bowlers. In doing so he drove that austere and redoubtable character nearly to distraction. In MCC's return match against Taylor's province of Natal, which brought them the only defeat of their tour, Barnes took his cap, threw it to the ground and stormed off the field, chuntering about the umpiring and muttering: 'It's Taylor, Taylor all the time.' In a low-scoring game Taylor made 91 and 100.

For those few months his batting was in a class of its own. On slower pitches, made of turf, he was less successful, if only comparatively so. He was of good average height, had a delightful disposition, an instinctively orthodox method and played right forward or right back, very late and very straight. Like many batsmen of that time, he seldom wore a batting glove on his top hand, even against Barnes.

97

Allan Anthony **Donald**

'. . . has helped to persuade the young of Afrikanderdom that sport does not begin and end with rugby football.'

For the first time for more than twenty years the greatest match-winning fast bowler in the world is not a West Indian. It is Allan Donald, a rangy Afrikaner who did more than anyone to help South Africa win twenty of the first fifty-three Test matches they played after returning from the cricketing wilderness in 1992.

The fastest white bowler of this century, if only for a short time in his career, was probably Frank Tyson, closely challenged by Harold Larwood, Ray Lindwall, Cuan MaCarthy, Jeff Thomson and Dennis Lillee. On occasions, Donald has been in the same bracket. In the last year or two, though, he has become concerned less with speed and more with subtlety. Off a shortened but still very powerful run-up, he has widened his repertoire and improved his control. His striking rate of a wicket every 47 balls remains exceptionally high, and when his rhythm is right he can do wonders with the ball.

With over 200 Test wickets, Donald is now drawing away from all other South African bowlers. He pitches a fuller, more constructive length than his West Indian counterparts, but shares their natural athleticism in the field. Together with Hansie Cronje, Kepler Wessels and Fanie de Villiers, he has helped to persuade the young of Afrikanerdom that sport does not begin and end with rugby football.

98

Stanley Joseph **McCabe**

'. . . needed a challenge to motivate him.'

Of the half-dozen or so most famous attacking innings played in Test cricket between the two world wars, Stan McCabe was responsible for three.

The first and perhaps the most dramatic was his 187 not out at Sydney in the body-line series; the second was his 189 not out against South Africa at Johannesburg in December 1935 and the third his 232 at a run a minute at Trent Bridge in 1938. The first and last were played on perfect batting pitches, the other on something more worn and torn. It was at Trent Bridge, when McCabe was in full cry, that Don Bradman said to his side: 'Take a good look at this. You may never see its like again.' McCabe's particular glory was the hook, which, played against bowling such as Larwood's at Sydney and Kenneth Farnes's at Trent Bridge, is the most vivid and thrilling stroke in the book.

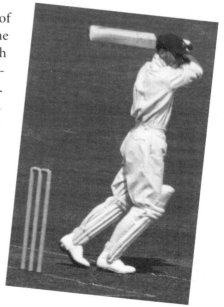

McCabe is one of a cluster of very fine cricketers to have come from up-country New South Wales. He had the build of a games-splayer and great natural ability. Sometimes, though, he needed a challenge to motivate him. Of his own bowling he thought too little: given the new ball from time to time, he used it at a briskish pace, and, being the wayward genius that he was, he startled the great Walter Hammond in the Oval Test match of 1930 by bowling him with an unrehearsed googly.

To anyone who used to sail with MCC sides to Australia and watch the one-day match against Ceylon when the ship berthed in Colombo, the islanders' talent for cricket, especially as wristy batsmen and twiddly bowlers, left a lasting impression. There was usually among them a batsman with a touch of genius – an embryonic Aravinda de Silva.

It is wonderful that now, as Sri Lanka, they are the one-day champions of the world. Their demolition of the high and mighty Australians in the World Cup final in Lahore in 1996 was a momentous event, and no one had more to do with it than de Silva. The smaller a batsman is the more difficult it becomes to drive the faster bowlers; yet at 5ft 3½ins de Silva not only drove Glenn McGrath and Paul Reiffel on that occasion, he steered them to within inches of where he wanted. And when he was not doing that, he was flicking the ball from off his off stump past the square-leg umpire. Sheer magic it was.

De Silva uses a bat with an unusually short handle and a very thick grip, and the pleasure he gives with it and gets from it is one of the game's greatest delights. Bats are his passion. His cricket bag is an Aladdin's Cave of bats and gloves. He lives, sleeps and exudes cricket, and plays it like a child of nature.

99

Pinnaduwage Aravinda
de Silva

'He lives, sleeps and exudes cricket . . .'

John Richard **Reid**

'. . . an immensely strong, completely natural and extraordinarily versatile cricketer.'

There can have been very few sides at any time that would not have been stronger and better balanced for having John Reid as a member. His lot, in fact, was to spend most of his career trying to make New Zealand sides competitive, often with little support of much substance.

He was an immensely strong, completely natural, extraordinarily versatile cricketer. A great hitter of the ball, an out-swing bowler, an off-break bowler, a one-time provincial wicket-keeper, a brilliant fielder and an irrepressible captain, he put it all together on New Zealand's tour to South Africa in 1961–62.

His 1,915 runs then, at an average of 68.39, are still a record for a South African season, and his efforts were crowned by New Zealand's first two victories overseas. In the second of them, at Port Elizabeth, Reid's bowling figures on the last day, with South Africa needing 314 to win, were 45 overs – 27 maidens – 44 runs – 4 wickets. Six years earlier, against West Indies at Auckland, he had led New Zealand to their first-ever Test victory, a moment of high and long-deferred emotion.

In 1963 Reid strewed an innings of 296 for Wellington against Northern Districts at the Basin Reserve ground in Wellington with fifteen sixes, a world record until Andrew Symonds hit sixteen for Gloucestershire against Glamorgan at Abergavenny in 1995.

Statistics (compiled by Robert Brooke)

Asterisk in highest score column denotes not out.

Figures for First-class and Test cricket apply until March 30 1998
and for One-day Internationals until April 24 1998

	MATCHES	INNINGS	NOT OUTS	RUNS	HIGHEST SCORE
1. WG Grace 1865–1908					
First-class cricket	879	1493	105	54896	344
Test Cricket	22	36	2	1098	170

(In some statistical circles there are arguments for alternative figures for WG Grace.
These are the traditional ones.)

	MATCHES	INNINGS	NOT OUTS	RUNS	HIGHEST SCORE
2. DG Bradman 1927–48					
First-class cricket	234	338	43	28067	452*
Test cricket	52	80	10	6996	334
3. GStA Sobers 1952/53–74					
First-class cricket	383	609	93	28315	365*
Test cricket	93	160	21	8032	365*
One-day Internationals	1	1	0	0	0
4. A Mynn 1832–59					
First-class cricket	212	395	26	4955	125*

741 wickets above – no analyses available.

	MATCHES	INNINGS	NOT OUTS	RUNS	HIGHEST SCORE
5. JB Hobbs 1905–34					
First-class cricket	825	1315	106	61237	316*
Test cricket	61	102	7	5410	211
6. SF Barnes 1894–1930					
First-class cricket	133	173	50	1573	93
Test cricket	27	39	9	242	38*
7. WR Hammond 1920–51					
First-class cricket	634	1005	104	50551	336*
Test cricket	85	140	16	7249	336*

AVERAGE	100S	CATCHES/ STUMPINGS	BALLS	WICKETS	AVERAGE
39.55	126	887	51545	2876	17.92
32.29	2	39	236	9	26.22
95.14	117	131/1	1367	36	37.97
99.94	29	32	72	2	36.00
54.87	86	407	28941	1043	27.74
57.78	26	109	7999	235	34.03
–	–	1	31	1	–
13.42	1	125	2989	292 +741	10.23
50.65	197	338	2682	107	25.06
56.94	15	17	165	1	–
12.78	–	72	12289	719	17.09
8.06	–	12	3106	189	16.43
56.10	167	819/3	22389	732	30.58
58.45	22	110	3138	83	37.80

	MATCHES	INNINGS	NOT OUTS	RUNS	HIGHEST SCORE
8. IVA Richards 1971/72–93					
First-class cricket	507	796	63	36212	322
Test cricket	121	182	12	8540	291
One-day Internationals	187	167	24	6721	189*
9. IT Botham 1974–93					
First-class cricket	402	617	46	19399	228
Test cricket	102	161	6	5200	208
One-day Internationals	116	106	15	2113	79
10. DCS Compton 1936–64					
First-class cricket	515	839	88	38942	300
Test cricket	78	131	15	5807	278
11. L Hutton 1934–60					
First-class cricket	513	814	91	40140	364
One-day Internationals	79	138	15	6971	364
12. FE Woolley 1906–38					
First-class cricket	979	1532	85	58969	305*
Test cricket	64	98	7	3283	154
13. SK Warne 1990/91–					
First-class cricket	123	160	23	2141	74*
Test cricket	67	93	10	1230	74*
One-day Internationals	96	56	17	469	55
14. VT Trumper 1894/95–1913/14					
First-class cricket	255	401	21	16939	300*
Test cricket	48	89	8	3163	214*
15. BA Richards 1964/65–82/83					
First-class cricket	339	576	58	28358	356
Test cricket	4	7	0	508	140
16. Imran Khan 1968/69–91/92					
First-class cricket	382	582	99	17771	170
Test cricket	88	126	25	3807	136
One-day Internationals	175	151	40	3709	102*

AVERAGE	100S	CATCHES/ STUMPINGS	BALLS	WICKETS	AVERAGE
49.40	114	464/1	10070	223	45.15
50.23	24	122	1964	32	61.37
47.00	11	101	4228	118	35.83
33.97	38	354	31902	1172	27.22
33.54	14	120	10878	383	28.40
23.21	–	36	4139	145	28.54
51.85	123	416	20074	622	32.27
50.06	17	49	1410	25	56.40
55.51	129	400	5106	173	29.51
56.67	19	57	232	3	77.33
40.75	145	1018	41066	2068	19.85
36.07	5	64	2815	83	33.91
15.62	–	77	13633	530	25.72
14.81	–	46	7756	313	24.73
12.02	–	34	3704	150	24.69
44.57	42	171	2008	64	31.37
39.04	8	31	317	8	39.62
54.74	80	367	2886	77	37.48
72.57	2	3	26	1	–
36.79	30	117	28726	1287	22.32
37.69	6	28	8258	362	22.81
33.41	1	37	4845	182	26.62

	MATCHES	INNINGS	NOT OUTS	RUNS	HIGHEST SCORE

17. KR Miller 1937/38–59
	MATCHES	INNINGS	NOT OUTS	RUNS	HIGHEST SCORE
First-class cricket	226	326	36	14183	281*
Test cricket	55	87	7	2958	147

18. R Benaud 1948/49–67/68
	MATCHES	INNINGS	NOT OUTS	RUNS	HIGHEST SCORE
First-class cricket	259	365	44	11719	187
Test cricket	63	97	7	2201	122

19. DK Lillee 1969/70–88
	MATCHES	INNINGS	NOT OUTS	RUNS	HIGHEST SCORE
First-class cricket	198	241	70	2377	73*
Test cricket	70	90	24	905	73*
One-day Internationals	63	34	8	240	42*

20. AV Bedser 1939–60
	MATCHES	INNINGS	NOT OUTS	RUNS	HIGHEST SCORE
First-class cricket	485	576	181	5735	126
Test cricket	51	71	15	714	79

21. GA Headley 1927/28–54
	MATCHES	INNINGS	NOT OUTS	RUNS	HIGHEST SCORE
First-class cricket	103	164	22	9921	344*
Test cricket	22	40	4	2190	270*

22. RR Lindwall 1941/42–61/62
	MATCHES	INNINGS	NOT OUTS	RUNS	HIGHEST SCORE
First-class cricket	228	270	39	5042	134*
Test cricket	61	84	13	1502	118

23. SM Gavaskar 1966/67–87
	MATCHES	INNINGS	NOT OUTS	RUNS	HIGHEST SCORE
First-class cricket	348	563	61	25834	340
Test cricket	125	214	16	10122	236*
One-day Internationals	108	102	14	3092	103*

24. ER Dexter 1956–68
	MATCHES	INNINGS	NOT OUTS	RUNS	HIGHEST SCORE
First-class cricket	327	567	48	21150	205
Test cricket	62	102	8	4502	205

25. SR Tendulkar 1988/89–
	MATCHES	INNINGS	NOT OUTS	RUNS	HIGHEST SCORE
First-class cricket	139	207	21	11181	204*
Test cricket	61	92	9	4552	179
One-day Internationals	188	182	16	6656	143

AVERAGE	100S	CATCHES/ STUMPINGS	BALLS	WICKETS	AVERAGE
48.90	41	136	11087	497	22.30
36.97	7	38	3906	170	22.97
36.50	23	254	23371	945	24.73
24.45	3	65	6704	248	27.03
13.90	–	67	20695	882	23.46
13.71	–	23	8493	355	23.92
9.23	–	10	2145	103	20.82
14.51	1	289	39279	1924	20.41
12.75	–	26	5876	236	24.89
69.86	33	76	1842	51	36.11
60.83	10	14	230	0	–
21.82	5	123	16956	794	21.35
21.15	2	26	5251	228	23.03
51.46	81	293	1240	22	56.36
51.12	34	108	206	1	–
35.13	1	22	25	1	–
40.75	51	233	12539	419	29.92
47.89	9	29	2306	66	34.93
60.11	34	96	1875	27	69.44
54.84	16	42	276	5	59.20
40.09	15	65	3282	62	52.93

	MATCHES	INNINGS	NOT OUTS	RUNS	HIGHEST SCORE
26. WJ O'Reilly 1927/28–45/46					
First-class cricket	135	167	41	1655	56*
Test cricket	27	39	7	410	56*
27. ED Weekes 1944/45–63/64					
First-class cricket	152	241	24	12010	304*
Test cricket	48	81	5	4455	207
28. BC Lara 1987/88–					
First-class cricket	140	229	7	11643	501*
Test cricket	54	91	3	4550	375
One-day Internationals	130	128	12	5448	169
29. RJ Hadlee 1971/72–90					
First-class cricket	342	473	93	12052	210*
Test cricket	86	134	19	3124	151*
One-day Internationals	115	98	17	1751	79
30. RG Pollock 1961/62–86/87					
First-class cricket	262	437	54	20940	274
Test cricket	23	41	4	2256	274
31. A Shrewsbury 1875–1902					
First-class cricket	498	813	90	26505	267
Test cricket	23	40	4	1277	164
32. FR Spofforth 1874/75–1897					
First-class cricket	155	236	41	1928	56
Test cricket	18	29	6	217	50
33. PBH May 1948–63					
First-class cricket	388	618	77	27592	285*
Test cricket	66	106	9	4537	285*
34. W Rhodes 1898–1930					
First-class cricket	1106	1528	237	39802	267*
Test cricket	58	98	21	2325	179
35. KS Ranjitsinhji 1893–1920					
First-class cricket	307	500	62	24692	285*
Test cricket	15	26	4	989	175

AVERAGE	100S	CATCHES/ STUMPINGS	BALLS	WICKETS	AVERAGE
13.13	–	65	12850	774	16.60
12.81	–	7	3254	144	22.59
55.34	36	125/1	731	17	43.00
58.61	15	49	77	1	–
52.44	37	182	315	2	157.50
51.70	10	75	28	0	–
46.92	12	62	34	2	17.00
31.71	14	198	26998	1490	18.11
27.16	2	39	9611	431	22.29
21.61	–	27	3407	158	21.56
54.67	64	248	2062	43	47.95
60.97	7	17	204	4	51.00
36.65	59	377	2	0	–
35.47	3	29	2	0	–
9.88	–	83	12760	853	14.95
9.43	–	11	1731	94	18.41
51.00	85	282	49	0	–
46.77	13	42	–	–	–
30.83	58	764	69993	4187	16.71
30.19	2	60	3425	127	26.96
56.37	72	233	4601	133	34.59
44.95	2	13	39	1	–

	MATCHES	INNINGS	NOT OUTS	RUNS	HIGHEST SCORE
36. FM Worrell 1941/42–64					
First-class cricket	208	326	49	15025	308*
Test cricket	51	87	9	3860	261
37. AR Border 1975/76–95/96					
First-class cricket	385	625	97	27131	205
Test cricket	156	265	44	11174	205
One-day Internationals	273	252	39	6524	127*
38. CL Walcott 1941/42–63/64					
First-class cricket	146	238	29	11820	314*
Test cricket	44	74	7	3798	220
39. W Beldham 1787–1821					
First-class cricket	196	359	22	7308	144

A small number of scores of great matches in which Beldham played are probably missing; also the total of wickets quoted refer only to those identified as being taken by Beldham in the scorecard. He almost certainly took many more wickets for which he was never credited.

	MATCHES	INNINGS	NOT OUTS	RUNS	HIGHEST SCORE
40. GA Lohmann 1884–96/97					
First-class cricket	293	427	39	7247	115
Test cricket	18	26	2	213	62*
41. GH Hirst 1891–1929					
First-class cricket	824	1215	151	36323	341
Test cricket	24	38	3	790	85
42. H Sutcliffe 1919–45					
First-class cricket	748	1088	123	50138	313
Test cricket	54	84	9	4555	194
43. MJ Procter 1965–88/89					
First-class cricket	401	667	58	21936	254
Test cricket	7	10	1	226	48
44. GS Chappell 1966/67–83/84					
First-class cricket	321	542	72	24535	247*
Test cricket	87	151	19	7110	247*
One-day Internationals	74	72	14	2331	138*

AVERAGE	100S	CATCHES/ STUMPINGS	BALLS	WICKETS	AVERAGE
54.24	39	139	10115	349	28.98
49.48	9	43	2672	69	38.72
51.38	70	379	4161	106	39.25
50.56	27	156	1525	39	39.10
30.62	3	127	2071	73	28.36
56.55	40	174/33	1269	35	36.25
56.68	15	53/11	408	11	37.09
21.68	3	345/49		222	
18.67	3	337	25295	1841	13.73
8.87	–	28	1205	112	10.75
34.13	60	607	51282	2739	18.72
22.57	–	18	1770	59	30.00
51.95	149	466	527	10	52.70
60.73	16	23			
36.01	48	325	27679	1417	19.53
25.11	–	4	616	41	15.02
52.20	74	376	8717	291	29.95
53.86	24	122	1913	47	40.70
40.18	3	23	2097	72	29.12

	MATCHES	INNINGS	NOT OUTS	RUNS	HIGHEST SCORE
45. FS Trueman 1949–69					
First-class cricket	603	713	120	9231	104
Test cricket	67	85	14	981	39*
46. HJ Tayfield 1945/46–62/63					
First-class cricket	187	259	47	3668	77
Test cricket	37	60	9	862	75
47. T Richardson 1892–1905					
First-class cricket	358	479	124	3424	69
Test cricket	14	24	8	177	25*
48. MC Cowdrey 1950–76					
First-class cricket	692	1130	134	42719	307
Test cricket	114	188	15	7624	182
49. Kapil Dev 1975/76–93/94					
First-class cricket	275	384	39	11356	193
Test cricket	131	184	15	5248	163
One-day Internationals	224	198	39	3783	175*
50. BS Bedi 1961/62–80/81					
First-class cricket	370	426	111	3584	61
Test cricket	67	101	28	656	50*
One-day Internationals	10	7	2	31	13
51. RN Harvey 1946/47–62/63					
First-class cricket	306	461	35	21699	231*
Test cricket	79	137	10	6149	205
52. RB Kanhai 1954/55–81/82					
First-class cricket	416	669	82	28774	256
Test cricket	79	137	6	6227	256
53. GA Gooch 1973–97					
First-class cricket	580	988	75	44841	333
Test cricket	118	215	6	8900	333
One-day Internationals	125	122	6	4290	142

AVERAGE	100S	CATCHES/ STUMPINGS	BALLS	WICKETS	AVERAGE
15.56	3	439	42154	2304	18.29
13.81	–	64	6605	307	21.57
17.30	–	149	18890	864	21.86
16.90	–	26	4405	170	25.91
9.64	–	126	38794	2104	18.43
11.06	–	5	2220	88	25.22
42.89	107	638	3329	65	51.21
44.06	22	120	104	0	–
32.91	18	192	22626	835	27.09
31.05	8	64	12687	434	29.64
23.79	1	71	6945	253	27.45
11.37	–	172	33843	1560	21.69
8.98	–	26	7637	266	28.71
6.20	–	4	340	7	48.57
50.93	67	228	1106	30	36.86
48.41	21	64	120	3	40.00
49.01	83	319/7	1009	18	56.05
47.53	15	50	85	0	–
49.11	128	555	8457	246	34.37
42.58	20	46	1069	23	46.47
36.98	8	45	1516	36	42.11

	MATCHES	INNINGS	NOT OUTS	RUNS	HIGHEST SCORE
54. CB Fry 1892–1921/22					
First-class cricket	394	658	43	30886	258*
Test cricket	26	41	3	1223	144
55. APE Knott 1964–85					
First-class cricket	511	745	134	18105	156
Test cricket	95	149	15	4389	135
One-day Internationals	20	14	4	200	50
56. AK Davidson 1949/50–62/63					
First-class cricket	193	246	39	6804	129
Test cricket	44	61	7	1328	80
57. KF Barrington 1953–68					
First-class cricket	533	831	136	31714	256
Test cricket	82	131	15	6806	256
58. Javed Miandad 1973/74–93/94					
First-class cricket	402	631	95	28647	311
Test cricket	124	189	21	8832	280*
One-day Internationals	233	218	41	7381	119*
59. IM Chappell 1961/62–79/80					
First-class cricket	262	448	41	19680	209
Test cricket	75	136	10	5345	196
One-day Internationals	16	16	2	673	86
60. Wasim Akram 1984/85–					
First-class cricket	204	280	33	5454	257*
Test cricket	79	109	15	2018	257*
One-day Internationals	247	194	36	2384	86
61. J Small					
First-class cricket	112	210	11	3582	136*

No details of catches or bowling available.

The above details have been compiled from all scores available to me. Only 3 of his scores have been traced before 1772, when he was already 35 years old.

AVERAGE	100S	CATCHES/ STUMPINGS	BALLS	WICKETS	AVERAGE
50.22	94	240	4872	166	29.34
32.18	2	17	3	0	–
29.63	17	1211/133	87	2	43.50
32.75	5	250/19			
20.00	–	15/1			
32.86	9	168	14048	672	20.90
24.59	–	42	3819	186	20.53
45.63	76	515	8907	273	32.62
58.67	20	58	1300	29	44.82
53.44	80	337/3	6395	191	33.48
52.57	23	93/1	682	17	40.11
41.70	8	71/2	297	7	42.42
48.35	59	312/1	6614	176	37.57
42.42	14	105	1316	20	65.80
48.07	–	5	23	2	11.50
22.08	5	69	18383	859	21.40
21.46	2	30	7706	341	22.59
15.08	–	59	8117	356	22.80
18.00	1				

	MATCHES	INNINGS	NOT OUTS	RUNS	HIGHEST SCORE
62. G Boycott 1962–86					
First-class cricket	609	1014	162	48426	261*
Test cricket	108	193	23	8114	246*
One-day Internationals	36	34	4	1082	105
63. AG Steel 1877–95					
First-class cricket	162	261	23	7000	171
Test cricket	13	20	3	600	148
64. TG Evans 1939–69					
First-class cricket	465	753	52	14882	144
Test cricket	91	133	14	2439	104
65. MA Holding 1972/73–89					
First-class cricket	222	283	43	3600	80
Test cricket	60	76	10	910	73
One-day Internationals	102	42	11	282	64
66. LN Constantine 1921/22–45					
First-class cricket	119	197	11	4475	133
Test cricket	18	33	0	635	90
67. CH Lloyd 1963/64–86					
First-class cricket	490	730	96	31232	242*
Test cricket	110	175	14	7515	242*
One-day Internationals	87	69	19	1977	102
68. CV Grimmett 1911/12–40/41					
First-class cricket	248	321	54	4720	71*
Test cricket	37	50	10	557	50
69. MD Marshall 1977/78–95/96					
First-class cricket	408	516	73	11004	120*
Test cricket	81	107	11	1810	92
One-day Internationals	136	83	19	955	66
70. JC Laker 1946–64/65					
First-class cricket	450	548	108	7304	113
Test cricket	46	63	15	676	63

AVERAGE	100S	CATCHES/ STUMPINGS	BALLS	WICKETS	AVERAGE
56.83	151	264	1459	45	32.42
47.72	22	33	382	7	54.57
36.06	1	5	105	5	21.00
29.41	8	137	11665	789	14.78
35.29	2	5	605	29	20.86
21.22	7	816/250	245	2	122.50
20.49	2	173/46			
15.00	–	125	18233	778	23.43
13.78	–	22	5898	249	23.68
9.09	–	30	3034	142	21.36
24.05	5	133	8991	439	20.48
19.24	–	28	1746	58	30.10
49.26	79	377	4104	114	36.00
46.67	19	90	622	10	62.20
39.54	1	39	210	8	26.25
17.67	–	139	31738	1424	22.28
13.92	–	17	5231	216	24.21
24.83	7	145	31548	1651	19.10
18.85	–	25	7876	376	20.94
14.92	–	15	4233	157	26.96
16.60	2	270	35791	1944	18.41
14.08	–	12	4101	193	21.24

	MATCHES	INNINGS	NOT OUTS	RUNS	HIGHEST SCORE
71. Waqar Younis 1987/88–					
First-class cricket	162	184	42	1818	55
Test cricket	53	69	12	556	45
One-day Internationals	171	85	31	537	37
72. DI Gower 1975–93					
First-class cricket	448	727	70	26339	228
Test cricket	117	204	18	8231	215
One-day Internationals	114	111	8	3170	158
73. CTB Turner 1882/83–1909/10					
First-class cricket	155	261	13	3856	103
Test cricket	17	32	4	323	29
74. AC MacLaren 1890–1922/23					
First-class cricket	424	703	52	22236	424
Test cricket	35	61	4	1931	140
75. GL Jessop 1894–1914					
First-class cricket	493	855	37	26698	286
Test cricket	18	26	0	569	104
76. A Shaw 1864–97					
First-class cricket	404	630	101	6585	88
(1 wkt for which no analysis)					
Test cricket	7	12	1	111	40
77. JB Statham 1950–68					
First-class cricket	559	647	145	5424	62
Test cricket	70	87	28	675	38
78. VAP van der Bijl 1967/68–82/83					
First-class cricket	156	188	48	2269	87
79. CG Macartney 1905/06–35/36					
First-class cricket	249	360	32	15019	345
Test cricket	35	55	4	2131	170

AVERAGE	100S	CATCHES/ STUMPINGS	BALLS	WICKETS	AVERAGE
12.80	–	38	15487	732	21.15
9.75	–	7	5748	267	21.52
9.94	–	19	6496	281	23.11
40.08	53	280/1	227	4	56.75
44.25	18	74	20	1	–
30.77	7	44	14	0	–
15.54	2	85	14157	993	14.25
11.53	–	8	1670	101	16.53
34.15	47	453	267	1	–
33.87	5	29	–	–	–
32.63	53	463	19904	873	22.79
21.88	1	11	354	10	35.40
12.44	–	368	24580	2027	12.12
10.09	–	4	285	12	23.75
10.80	–	230	36999	2260	16.37
11.44	–	28	6261	252	24.84
16.20	–	51	12692	767	16.54
45.78	49	102	8781	419	20.95
41.78	7	17	1240	45	27.55

	MATCHES	INNINGS	NOT OUTS	RUNS	HIGHEST SCORE
80. RB Simpson 1952/53–77/78					
First-class cricket	257	436	62	21029	359
Test cricket	62	111	7	4869	311
One-day Internationals	2	2	0	36	23
81. CEL Ambrose 1985/86–					
First-class cricket	212	272	64	3063	78
Test cricket	80	114	22	1188	53*
One-day Internationals	151	81	34	540	31*
82. Fazal Mahmood 1943/44–63/64					
First-class cricket	111	146	33	2602	100*
Test cricket	34	50	6	620	60
83. WH Ponsford 1920/21–34/35					
First-class cricket	162	235	23	13819	437
Test cricket	29	48	4	2122	266
84. Hanif Mohammad 1951/52–75/76					
First-class cricket	238	370	44	17059	499
Test cricket	55	97	8	3915	337
85. FS Jackson 1890–1907					
First-class cricket	309	505	35	15901	160
Test cricket	20	33	4	1415	144*
86. RGD Willis 1969–84					
First-class cricket	308	333	145	2690	72
Test cricket	90	128	55	840	28*
One-day Internationals	64	22	14	83	24
87. WW Armstrong 1898/99–1921/22					
First-class cricket	269	406	61	16158	303*
Test cricket	50	84	10	2863	159*
88. DL Underwood 1963–87					
First-class cricket	676	710	200	5165	111
Test cricket	86	116	35	937	45*
One-day Internationals	26	13	4	53	17

AVERAGE	100S	CATCHES/ STUMPINGS	BALLS	WICKETS	AVERAGE
56.22	60	383	13287	349	38.07
46.81	10	110	3001	71	42.26
18.00	–	4	95	2	47.50
14.72	–	83	17167	839	20.46
13.20	–	16	7133	337	21.16
11.48	–	38	4721	204	23.14
23.02	1	38	8792	460	19.11
14.09	–	11	3434	139	24.70
65.18	47	71	41	0	–
48.22	7	21			
52.32	55	178/12	1509	53	28.47
43.98	12	40	95	1	–
33.83	31	195	15767	774	20.37
48.79	5	10	799	24	33.29
14.30	–	134	22468	899	24.99
11.50	–	39	8190	325	25.20
10.37	–	22	1968	80	24.60
46.83	45	273	16405	832	19.71
38.68	6	44	2923	87	33.59
10.12	1	261	49993	2465	20.28
11.56	–	44	7674	297	25.83
5.88	–	6	734	32	22.93

	MATCHES	INNINGS	NOT OUTS	RUNS	HIGHEST SCORE
89. S Ramadhin 1949/50–65					
First-class cricket	184	191	65	1092	44
Test cricket	43	58	14	361	44
90. LR Gibbs 1953/54–75/76					
First-class cricket	330	352	150	1729	43
Test cricket	79	109	39	488	25
One-day Internationals	3	1	1	0	0*
91. WW Hall 1955/56–70/71					
First-class cricket	170	215	38	2673	102*
Test cricket	48	66	14	818	50*
92. V Mankad 1935/36–61/62					
First-class cricket	233	361	27	11591	231
Test cricket	44	72	5	2109	231
93. H Larwood 1924–38					
First-class cricket	361	438	72	7289	102*
Test cricket	21	28	3	485	98
94. JM Gregory 1919–28/29					
First-class cricket	129	173	18	5659	152
Test cricket	24	34	3	1146	119
95. SR Waugh 1984/85–					
First-class cricket	251	383	65	16547	216*
Test cricket	103	162	29	6480	200
One-day Internationals	245	222	44	5639	102*
96. HW Taylor 1960–84					
First-class cricket	639	880	167	12065	100
Test cricket	57	83	12	1156	97
One-day Internationals	27	17	7	130	26*
97. AA Donald 1985/86–					
First-class cricket	253	295	112	2242	55*
Test cricket	42	57	21	398	33
One-day Internationals	102	24	10	55	11

AVERAGE	100S	CATCHES/ STUMPINGS	BALLS	WICKETS	AVERAGE
8.66	–	38	15345	758	20.24
8.20	–	9	4579	158	28.98
8.55	–	203	27878	1024	27.22
6.97	–	52	8989	309	29.09
–	–	–	59	2	29.50
15.10	1	58	14273	546	26.14
15.73	–	11	5066	192	26.38
34.70	26	190	19183	782	24.53
31.47	5	33	5236	162	32.32
19.91	3	234	24994	1427	17.51
19.40	–	15	2212	78	28.35
36.50	13	195	10580	504	20.99
36.96	2	37	2648	85	31.15
52.03	47	213	7600	240	31.66
48.72	14	77	3036	86	35.30
31.67	1	84	6285	184	34.15
16.92	1	1473/176	75	1	–
16.28	–	167/7	6	0	–
13.00	–	26/6			
12.25	–	97	22352	1004	22.26
11.05	–	11	4580	204	22.45
3.92	–	14	3600	171	21.46

	MATCHES	INNINGS	NOT OUTS	RUNS	HIGHEST SCORE
98. SJ McCabe 1928/29–1941/42					
First-class cricket	182	262	20	11951	240
Test cricket	39	62	5	2748	232
99. PA de Silva 1983/84–					
First-class cricket	173	272	27	12008	267
Test cricket	70	122	9	4852	267
One-day Internationals	233	226	24	7237	145
100. JR Reid 1947/48–65					
First-class cricket	246	418	28	16128	296
Test cricket	58	108	5	3428	142

AVERAGE	100S	CATCHES/ STUMPINGS		BALLS	WICKETS	AVERAGE
49.38	29	139		5362	159	33.72
48.21	6	41		1543	36	42.86
49.01	36	93		2626	74	35.48
42.93	16	37		806	20	40.30
35.82	10	73		2947	79	37.30
41.35	39	240/7		10535	466	22.60
33.28	6	43/1		2835	85	33.35

Acknowledgements

Archibald J. Stuart Wortley, 1890; 1

The Hulton Getty Picture Collection; 2a, 11, 12, 15, 17a, 17b, 18, 20, 21, 22b, 26, 27a, 27b, 30, 31, 33, 34, 35, 37, 38, 42, 45b, 46, 47, 49, 51a, 51b, 56, 64a, 66a, 66b, 68a, 70a, 73, 82, 83, 84, 88b, 89a, 89b, 91b, 93a, 93b, 94, 96, 98a, 98b, 100a, 100b.

Photographs by Patrick Eagar; 3a, 3b, 8, 13, 14, 16a, 16b, 19, 24, 25, 28, 29, 36, 43a, 43b, 44, 48a, 48b, 54, 55a, 57, 58, 59, 60, 67, 69a, 69b, 71, 72, 78, 80, 86, 90, 95, 99.

MCC Collection; 4, 40, 62, 85b.

Ken Kelly; 6, 9a, 9b, 23, 50, 52, 63b, 88, 97.

Alpha/S&G; 10, 45a, 70b.

David Frith; 22a, 76.

The Mansell Collection/Time Inc/Katz; 32,

A. Vincent c.1860; 39.

C. W. Alcock; 53.

All Sport; 63a, 65, 75.

Roy Ullyett; 64b.

A. A. Mailey; 79.

Photograph by David Munden/Sportsline Photographic; 81b.

The George Beldam Collection; 85a.

Reproduced by permission of Punch Ltd; 87.

PA News; 92.

The above numbers refer to each listed cricketer a) denotes a full page photograph and b) an inset where two photographs are featured per cricketer.

Every effort has been made to trace all copyright holders but if any has been inadvertently overlooked, the author and publishers will be pleased to make the necessary arrangement at first opportunity.